8-80

LIVING ON THE
PLUS SIDE

LIVING ON THE PLUS SIDE

JEANETTE LOCKERBIE

MOODY PRESS

CHICAGO

The use of selected references from various versions of the
Bible in this publication does not necessarily imply publisher
endorsement of the versions in their entirety.

Library of Congress Cataloging in Publication Data

Lockerbie, Jeanette W.
  Living on the plus side.
  Bibliography: p.
  1. Christian life—1960- I. Title.

BV4501.2.L625   248'.4   79-26440

ISBN 0-8024-9819-1

Printed in the United States of America

*To my good friend
George,
who knows how to
live on the plus side*

CONTENTS

CHAPTER   PAGE

Acknowledgments   11

Introduction   13

1. You Can Get There from Here: The Plus of
   Being Able to Change   15

2. There's Just One You: The Plus of Being Who
   You Are   25

3. Magnetic Christianity: The Plus of a Joy-filled
   Life   35

4. A Packet of Possibilities: The Plus of Good
   Expectations   45

5. But 490 Times: The Plus of a Forgiving Spirit   53

6. You Can't Go It Alone: The Plus of Being
   Both a Giver and a Receiver   63

7. You *Can* Do Something Well: The Plus of
   Achievement   71

8. Why Doesn't God *Do* Something?: The Plus
   of Acceptance   83

9. Serene and Satisfied: The Plus of a Contented
   Spirit   97

10. Expression or Repression: The Plus of
    Balanced Emotions   109

11. Under His Wings: The Plus of Inner Security   121

12. But You Don't Understand: The Plus of an
    Understanding Heart   135

13. Living Is for Now: The Plus of the Present   147

ACKNOWLEDGMENTS

Acceptance Spells Peace, Jeanette W. Lockerbie. Used with permission of the Narramore Christian Foundation, Rosemead, California 91770.

"One Day at a Time," Annie Johnson Flint. Used with permission of Evangelical Publishers, Toronto, Ontario, Canada M5C 2M5.

Tomorrow's at My Door, Jeanette W. Lockerbie. Used with permission of Fleming H. Revell Company, Old Tappan, New Jersey 07675.

"God Holds the Key of All Unknown," from *Sankey's Sacred Songs and Solos.* Used with kind permission of Marshall, Morgan, and Scott Publications, Ltd., London, England EC1V9LB.

"In Acceptance Lieth Peace," from *Toward Jerusalem,* Amy Carmichael. Used with permission of Christian Literature Crusade, Fort Washington, Pennsylvania 19034.

INTRODUCTION

"You can't get there from here" is a quip that portrays a presumed impossibility or a shrug-the-shoulders "I give up" stance.

Too often the same philosophy is applied to our attitudes. I admit to having been a bit of a "bandwagoner" concerning the impossibility of changing attitudes.

I had been a Christian for a number of years before I began to see the utter incongruity of nonjoyful, poor-expectations Christianity. Yet that was characteristic of me much of the time. I was negative in my thinking, and critical. To criticize is always so easy—it takes hardly any skill at all.

And catastrophic expectations? I was right in there.

Controlled by "What will 'they' think?" I envied the free souls who could afford to be themselves.

Though I knew by memory many of the strong promises of God, though I likewise realized that His promises are "yea and . . . Amen" in Christ Jesus, I lived with a host of insecurities. I did not know God's assurances by *heart*—by standing on the promises and finding myself on firm ground.

But I am learning. I am steadily moving from the minus column to the plus.

I would not want to present to my readers something I have not tried and found good. Otherwise I might be holding out a mirage, a cruel impossibility, false hope.

You *can* get there.

Mostly, change in attitude is not sudden or dramatic. Rather, it shows in quiet little triumphs in daily life. And it has to do with choices: I can be negative or positive in my outlook; I can be harsh, rigid, cold—or warm, flexible, and cooperative; I can be critical—or I can choose to be compassionate; I can be doggedly unforgiving—or I can know the bliss of having a forgiving spirit (even if it means 490 times).

Another valuable truth the Lord has taught me is that I will never change, never learn, *when my mind is closed*.

It is a journey from the minus to the plus side. There are hurdles of hopelessness and hills and valleys of up-and-down experiences. But it need not always be a one-step-forward-and-two-backward frustration. Let me encourage you that you can make progress. The journey is well worth the trouble, for the plus side is always the winner's circle.

1

YOU CAN GET THERE FROM HERE:

The Plus of Being Able to Change

A plus always presupposes an already present level or amount.

Likewise, a plus calls for *and provides* a new total.

We can apply that premise to our Christian lives, for at all times we are in a certain state. But we do not have to remain there.

How often we hear the quip "You can't get there from here." Usually it is facetious and concerns locations and directions.

Sadly, we hear it when it is not so funny, when the person means it and it has more importance than how to get from here to there in the physical sense. I have heard those words said with regard to the possibility of change and growth in a Christian.

Some people view themselves as hopeless as far as ever changing and gaining a plus level in the matter of their attitudes and behavior is concerned.

To be sure, the Bible asks if the leopard can change his spots. But we are not leopards. We can do something about our "spots."

15

I was not always that positive. For too many years my own attitudes were virtually stuck in cement. I was almost totally negative in my thinking, and it would have been difficult for anyone to persuade me that I could change.

I feel somewhat qualified, then, to assure you that you can change. You can "get there from here." And how gratifying when someone who has known us for a long time says, "You've changed—and I like you better this way."

Perhaps we need to evaluate the greeting "You haven't changed a bit!" To illustrate, Linda and Marie had not seen each other for a number of years. Suddenly they came face to face at a convention, and after they had greeted one another warmly, Marie took a step back and admiringly appraised her former neighbor. Then, with utmost sincerity in her voice she exclaimed, "You haven't changed one bit, Linda!"

It is a common enough scene at high school and college reunions, at organizational functions, or when two people meet just by chance after a period of separation.

Another aspect of "You haven't changed" is seen when the phrase is loaded with negative connotations. Built into it may be the implication that the one spoken of still has the same old undesirable traits: the same tendency to talk all the time, or to gossip or to criticize continually—or other characteristics that guarantee a zero popularity rating.

More than likely the person *has* changed; the traits are stronger than ever. It is a fact of life that we do not remain static; for good or bad, we change. That is, however, a hope-filled truth for as long as we are alive we have the opportunity to improve in many areas of our lives.

16

THE RIGHTNESS OF CHANGE

Why should you, why should I be interested in taking steps toward change?

The primary reason is that *God* is for it.

Fortunately for us, the Lord does not require that we change in order for Him to save us and take us into His family. But He does look for change in us following conversion. God's stated aspiration for us is given in 2 Corinthians 3:18: "Beholding . . . the glory of the Lord, [we] are changed . . . even as by the Spirit of the Lord."

That being so, why should we ever set store by, or feel complimented by, someone's saying to us, "You haven't changed one little bit"?

If we have not changed, we have not grown.

Nature affirms that God is for change. We see that in the seasons of the year, in the unfolding of a leaf, in the opening of a rosebud. We marvel at the metamorphosis of the chrysalis into the butterfly.

Does it not, then, follow that God would have a design for creative change in us, His highest creation?

The Bible teaches that God's ideal for believers is that we move on from milk to meat in our normal progress from "baby Christian" to maturing member of His Body (Hebrews 5:12-14).

Without *change* there can be no *growth*.

THE BENEFITS OF CHANGE

Perhaps, if we would admit it, many of us are at the core not satisfied with our spiritual condition. And that is not such a bad feeling—unless we stop there. It can be an impetus toward something better. That dissatisfaction with

17

ourselves might be called "divine discontent." It is not a lack of contentment with what God sends into our lives. Rather, I think of it as a driving desire to move on, to know Him better, to serve Him more wholeheartedly. Ultimately that discontent will help us to grow more into the image of God's dear Son.

We may not have verbalized that feeling of spiritual dissatisfaction. We may just vaguely sense it. But Paul has put it into words for us in Philippians 3:12-14: "Not as though I had already attained, either were already perfect: but I follow after. . . . I count not myself to have apprehended: but this one thing I do . . . I press toward the mark."

In our pressing toward the mark, there is a great benefit. In the doing of it, we have the good inner feeling that we are on the right track, that we are pursuing God's course for us. At times it may seem we are taking one step forward and two backward. We will know discouragement. But the compensation will be in realizing that with the Lord's help we are gradually changing in the right direction.

You may wish to list the benefits—big and little—that you realize as you "press toward the mark for the prize of the high calling of God in Christ Jesus." It will help, also, if you have a prayer partner venturing on the same course; you will encourage each other by prayer and the sharing of your experiences.

What Change Entails

The first step toward change in any aspect of one's life is facing up to the *need* for such change. I am no advocate of change for change's sake.

Second, it is good to check up on ourselves periodically,

as objectively as possible. Unless we do, we can become victims of the "as it was in the beginning, is now and ever shall be" syndrome—that in contrast to our being willing to assess, then—when necessary—to do some rearranging of our lives. To quote Dr. Raymond C. Ortlund, "Some of us suffer hardening of the categories." We need not, if we will "judge ourselves" as the Scripture exhorts us (1 Corinthians 11:31). What we see in the mirror of God's Word can motivate us toward change, so that is another step.

A sign of change in ourselves might be noticed in our attitude toward change in another person. Seemingly we can more easily trust the Holy Spirit to effect change in us than in those around us. We may tend to think, *Oh, he won't change,* or *I'd never expect her to change.* It is a mark of growth when we come to have at least as high expectations of the other person as we have of ourselves. Without that, we might have to question whether we are spiritually smug.

Because we can look only on the outside, we should resist the temptation to compare our own growth and progress with that of others *to their disadvantage.*

It is good when we can genuinely pray, "Lord, You know that I'm not yet what I want to be; but I do thank You that I'm not what I used to be," and then happily move on toward even more inner change.

Growth is indicated when we ask ourselves, *"What prevents me from changing?"*

Let us look at some obvious hindrances.

• *Lack of recognition of our present state (the unexamined life).* We never move toward a desired "there" until we realize where "here" is. That makes me think of the giant

19

shopping malls. Sometimes in one of those I am totally confused as to how to find what I am looking for. Fortunately, I spot a directory and map. Now I know where the various stores are located. But is that enough to solve my problem? No. What does set me straight is that arrow superimposed on the map and the words "You are *here*." Knowing where *I am* in that maze of stores, I can figure which way to turn to find where *I want to go*. So it is in our bid for a changed life.

• *Complacency.* I think of that as my knowing where I am and being perfectly satisfied to stay there: no *desire* to change. That is the reverse of "divine discontent."

• *Hostility.* Sometimes hostility is evidenced in words such as, "I'm just what God made me; I am what I am, and nobody's going to change me." Could this express a defiant attitude? Does the person who feels so hostile also feel absolved of all responsibility to become more lovable, or compassionate, or charitable—or to change in any way for the better?

• *Unrealistic goals.* That deterrent to positive change speaks of the over optimistic individual. He sets goals toward improvement beyond his ability to achieve. For instance, the nagging wife may determine, "I'll *never again* nag." The habitually late person may say, "I'm *never* going to be late again as long as I live." Generally such persons, though honest in their intent, are promising too much, too soon. Then, when they cannot reach their unrealistic goals, they feel like failures, become discouraged, and give up trying to change.

• *Poor expectations.* "I tried it before, and it doesn't work. Finally, but most important,

20

• *Failure to cooperate with the Holy Spirit.* That failure is rooted in unbelief, the exact opposite of "I can do all things through Christ which strengtheneth me" (Philippians 4:13).

How Do We Proceed Toward Change?

Because God has made us all different, our progress toward change will follow a variety of patterns and involve different types of people and experiences.

Personally, I am indebted to some people who, day after day, rubbed me the wrong way, for one reason or another. That has had the effect of smoothing many a rough corner of my personality. How has that been accomplished? It has taken place as I have sought the Lord for grace not to "blow my stack." From there, it has been a growing, maturing change process. I decided I was really beginning to move in the right direction when I could objectively appraise the other person's irksome behavior, then ask myself, *Could it be that my actions are doing the same thing to Mary that her actions are doing to me? that maybe, she is praying for grace to put up with me?*

Many times, when I am irritated almost beyond measure, my prayer is: "Lord, please—I don't want to do the same thing to her that she's doing to me. I know You're using it to sandpaper my rough spots. But I don't want You to use me to sandpaper other people. I wouldn't want that ministry."

As long as we are in the world and in the company of other people there will inevitably be those who irk us to some degree. And let me say that much of that may be quite unintentional on the part of the other people. They may be totally unaware of what certain quirks, mannerisms, or hab-

21

its are doing to the people who have to put up with them. Whatever the problem—and usually it is an insignificant thing in itself—if it causes us to stop and question our own actions and attitudes, it is a good thing, and the offending person has done us a great favor.

When through such insights we recognize our own irritating traits, the sooner we take steps to correct them, the better. The younger we are, the less painful change is. As we get older, it is less easy to bend without breaking. We become brittle, and change—however minor—can be a major problem for us. So today is the best of all days for self-evaluation and a step toward change.

Note: I did not suggest self-change. We do not have to "go it alone" when we are endeavoring to do what the Holy Spirit is leading us to do. That is one of the "all things" the Bible speaks of in Philippians 4:13.

How Willing Am I to Change?

Change involves an act of the will.

It follows, then, that no matter how *dissatisfied* we are with our present state, no matter how much *insight* we have as to the need for change, that is not enough. We have to be willing. Having faced up to the need, we can ask God to help us to be willing to move toward change and growth. God is more willing to help us than we are to be helped, so we can confidently count on His enabling us.

The next step, then, is to get down to specifics. A little questionnaire like the following is often useful.

Am I willing to be less critical?
Am I willing to be more thankful and contented with what God gives me?

Am I willing to become less self-centered?

Am I willing to do something about my procrastinating?

Am I willing to stop excusing myself and blaming other people?

Am I willing to quit gossiping?

Am I willing to give up always having to be right in a disagreement?

Am I willing to go the "other mile"?

Being willing to change is the only requirement for exercising the plus of being able to change.

We may have to ask, Do I have any desire or willingness to change?

What if the answer is no?

Built into such resistance we might find a that's-how-we-did-it-last-year element. The implication is that there is not, nor can there be, a better way. So why change? I have heard this attitude described as "the skull and crossbones of creativity," and it surely is. Worse, such thinking is on a collision course with God's intent in the ever-changing pattern that is life.

Why not take a fresh look at where you are and where you desire to be in your ongoing walk with the Lord. Then, believing you *can* get from here to there, press on in the strength that He gives. It is not enough just to sing, "I'm pressing on the upward way," when you can know the joy and fulfillment of, "New heights I'm gaining every day."*

That is the end result of the plus of being able to change.

*"Higher Ground," by Johnson Oatman, Jr.

2

THERE'S JUST ONE YOU:
The Plus of Being Who You Are

"Just be yourself." How many times have you heard that piece of advice given? Generally it is offered to help allay the apprehension of a diffident person who is about to confront a new situation or meet new people. The assumption is that by "just being yourself" one is likely to be able to handle the situation or that "people will like you better."

Significantly, the counsel to "be yourself" is most often given to the very person who has a hard time being himself, for one reason or another.

I have heard more than one person say, "How can I be myself? *I don't know who I am.*"

"Nonsense," you may be saying, "everybody knows who he is."

That is normally true, in one sense. However, knowing who you are and having a sense of your own identity are two very different things. And it is the latter that gives some people a lot of problems. I do not recall that was much of a concern in earlier years. People were not wandering through life in search of their identities, trying to answer for themselves the question, "Who am I?" Yet, if I do not know who I am, how am I going to "be myself"?

First, then, each has to know that he has a "self," that he is not just one of the crowd. Moreover, he needs to recognize his own uniqueness.

Have you ever thought of the care God has taken to make each one of us different, even to our fingerprints? We may have the same parents and grandparents, we may live in the same house on the same street in the same town and be almost totally different one from the other. God does not deal in carbon copies, in "cookie cutter" people. Each of us is a unique creation.

Doesn't that make you feel special? I got so excited over that truth that I wrote these lines:

> I'm special to God
> There is only one me
> I lift my head high at the prospect.
> Not a piece or a pawn
> I'm a part of God's plan
> The blueprint He holds, the design He'll reveal
> One step at a time
> As I yield to His will . . .
> Yes, I'm *special* to God.

Surely, we can find our identities in being so special to God.

Some seem to get all their sense of identity through other people. They will keep us longer than we care to listen as they expound on their family trees. Others satisfy themselves that somebody in the family is important, even though they belittle themselves as being "nobodies."

GOD WANTS YOU TO BE YOU

Because God has made us different, we do whatever we do with that special something that is ours alone. God has made us *for* something; we are here with a God-ordained something to do (see Ephesians 2:10). Whether we are aware of it or not, we leave our stamp on our efforts, whatever the direction. The past few months I have been interested in following the hobby some of my friends have taken up. They are painting. Their instructor requires that for a time each pupil does the same project, and she gives the same instruction to each one. Yet, without fail, when those friends show their work, the differences are marked. The landscape or still life is the same, if you stop at noticing just what it is. But it does not take much scrutiny to see the differences. Each has added her own individual touch. The same is true of two people playing the same piece of music. Ask five people to write a description of the same thing, and you will get five different viewpoints. Why all those variances in seemingly the "same" things? The human element of uniqueness is the explanation. In writing, we call it *style*—and style comes from the inside. It is the *you* that comes through in what you do.

Since the Lord has made us one of a kind, and since He has ordained a particular thing for each to do, if we will not "be ourselves," that thing will *never* be done as God wants it done. For there is only one you, only one person in all the world who can do "your thing" in your unique way.

You Do Not Have to Be Somebody Else

I have heard people say, "I wish I were . . . [some other other person]." That is often just a momentary feeling and has an immediate cause. For example, we might wish we had something another person has. But that is not what I have in mind. Rather, I am referring to an individual who is constantly unhappy, not because of what he has or has not but because of who he *is* in his own eyes.

One day I was discussing that subject with Eileen, a young

27

woman who had told me she wished she were somebody else.

"Why don't you like being yourself?" I asked her.

She did not have to think long. "Because *I don't like myself.*" She emphasized each word with a stamp of her foot.

It was not hard to see that here was an unhappy girl. And being someone else, even if she could have made the transformation, would not have solved her problem. Eileen was looking for help. I was no expert, but I know Someone who is. I prayed therefore for a key to help Eileen unlock her dislike of herself, and the Lord gave me this idea:

"What kind of person *do* you like?" I asked, as there is no use in arguing with a person in that frame of mind.

"Oh." She thought for a few seconds, then enumerated the things she liked in other people. "And while I'm at it," she added, "I might as well tell you what makes people not like me, too."

I shall capsule both of her lists.

• What I like best in other people:

I like people who make me feel comfortable when I am with them.

I like people who accept me and let me be myself.

I like people who do not make me feel stupid when I am with them.

I like it when a person will really listen to me and let me do some of the talking.

• I feel people do not like me because:

I am not pretty.

I cannot carry on an interesting conversation with people.

I am shy—maybe afraid of people.

I come across as sort of stupid, so nobody wants to be with me much.

Eileen wanted to talk further, and some things soon became plain to her. She saw that although being pretty had seemed a cause for liking or not liking, it was not on the list of things she herself liked in another person. "So maybe it's not all that important," she concluded. As for her poor conversational skills, she learned that *listening* and *letting the other talk* was higher in her own priorities. Shyness? I could help her with that for I had suffered from being hopelessly shy much of my life. So I told her that shyness is generally rooted in deep insecurity, and that it can also be a kind of escape mechanism to keep one from taking risks. "If I don't play the game, I won't lose." "If I don't reach out to someone, I don't risk rejection." Her need for acceptance *as she was,* tied in with her feeling that she "comes across as stupid." It is understandable that she would be drawn to people who made her feel comfortable, who let her be herself without criticizing her.

It will take time, but I believe that Eileen—and others who "don't like themselves"—can change.

I showed Eileen that Christians are the most accepted people on earth, that "we are accepted in the beloved" (Ephesians 1:6), and that God who created her *to be herself,* accepted her as she was.

Eileen told me she would look in the mirror and say to herself, "I don't like you, Eileen." Now all that has stopped.

Why shouldn't we like ourselves, especially when we have discovered who we are in the sight of God?

For the past decade we have been hearing in a new way,

29

"Love your neighbor as yourself," with emphasis on "as yourself."

I have to admit that for much of my Christian life I skipped lightly over the latter part of that command, never having heard it expounded in the light in which I now see it. But as I began to move in Christian circles where the healthy concept of loving oneself *scripturally* is an accepted truth, I readily recognized it as a sound concept. For, when we love (accept, respect) *ourselves* as made in the image of God, so precious to Him that He gave His Son to save us from our sin, we can begin to love other people. Conversely, when we do not love ourselves (in the sense I have described), we have little love to give a neighbor.

You may be thinking, "It's one thing to love a person; but I can't always like the person." That reminds me of a missionary guest we had with us for dinner one time. Speaking of his brother, also a missionary on the same station, he said, "I love my brother Paul. But apart from that, I like the guy."

We can both love and like ourselves. A day or so ago, I was pleased to read this little item in a church bulletin: "God has liked me into liking myself."

So *who* are you? Someone unique whom God both loves and likes. *There* is an unbeatable source of identity.

(I should interject right here that *not everybody is going to like you*. But that should not be a reason for you to give up on liking yourself or to wish to be someone else.)

One way you can score yourself on your improvement, if you have been one who has never liked yourself, is to check your immediate response when you are given a compliment. Do you feel embarrassed? Apologetic? Do not know how to respond? Or can you feel comfortable in hearing something nice about yourself?

It is true that we have been exhorted not to think of ourselves more highly than we ought (Romans 12:3; note that word "more.") J. B. Phillips paraphrases that verse, "Don't cherish exaggerated ideas of yourself or your importance, but try to have a sane estimate of your capabilities."

We demean ourselves as God's masterpieces—worse, we in essence criticize the God who made us who and what we are—when we do not like ourselves and underestimate ourselves.

As believers, we have *everything* "going for us" if we will only believe that and function accordingly. Why then can we not just view ourselves as *God* sees us—then go ahead and *be ourselves.*

If, however, you still believe that you do not or cannot love or like yourself, it would be good to analyze why you think as you do. You can then take steps to handle the situation and to begin to change in the right direction. It is even possible to become, eventually, the person someone else sees as "the one I really like."

A Higher Aspiration

We have been considering our unique creation and what recognizing this can do for us.

But God did not stop at making you and me who we are. He holds up for us an infinitely more wonderful possibility. We can grow into the image of His own dear Son. Well might we sing:

> O to be like Thee! blessed Redeemer,
> This is my constant longing and prayer.

Gladly I'll forfeit all of earth's treasures,
Jesus, Thy perfect likeness to wear.

.   .   .   .

Come in Thy sweetness, come in Thy fullness;
Stamp Thine own image deep on my heart.

THOMAS O. CHISHOLM

But I am of the opinion that, magnificent as that prospect is, until we can feel free to "be ourselves" we may never even desire to follow on to this greater identification with our Lord Jesus Christ.

So it would appear that the positive, liberating "being who we are" has broad ramifications.

"Ye shall know the truth, and the truth shall make you free," Jesus said (John 8:32). The truth of who I am in God's sight—and His eternal purpose for me—encourages me to strive to be in a measure like Him.

What is God's ultimate purpose in saving us from our sin? I heard that question discussed at length while driving with a carload of people to a meeting. The speaker was in our car, and it was he who posed the question. Some of the answers came quick and with confidence that they were correct; others answered more thoughtfully. After listening to a number of answers, the Bible teacher commented on them kindly, then stated, "God's purpose in saving you and me is that He might conform us to the image of His son" (Romans 8:29). I never forgot that answer.

Paul gave the early church (and us) a clear, simple analogy as to how believers become increasingly like their Lord: "We all, with open face beholding as in a glass the glory of the Lord, are changed into the same image" (2 Corinthians 3:18).

32

The day is coming when *we shall be like Jesus.* The Bible tells us so in 1 John 3:2: "When he shall appear, we shall be like him."

Meanwhile, how can we be reaching our God-given potential? One way is by *knowing who we are, being what we are,* and doing that for which God has made us. We will do that best as we keep in mind that there is *just one of each of us.*

3

MAGNETIC CHRISTIANITY:

The Plus of a Joy-filled Life

Think of the word *joy*. Does it bring to mind a particular person? *Joy* immediately makes me envision a radiant young woman I met some time ago. She was leading the singing at a women's retreat. Observing her vibrancy, enthusiasm, and warmth, I thought, *How could anyone keep from singing with such a magnetic leader?* As the days went on I learned that here was a Christian woman who knew the joy of the Lord *in spite of tragedy and trials.* Hers was no surface, "pumped-up," bubbly disposition; rather, she had the buoyancy that comes from inner strength. And she was a tonic for everyone around her.

By contrast, in my area there is a man—I shall call him Sam Jones—who is well known as a devout Christian. When we had an earthquake recently some people were heard to say, "I wouldn't mind being in old Sam's shoes right now." But for the most part they view Sam and his Christianity as a gloomy scene. Frequently he says, "Nobody knows the joy I have 'way down in my heart." One day, frustrated by his perpetually somber appearance and attitude, I said, "Sam, why don't you get some of that joy up where people can see it?"

In one sense that man has a good testimony. Everyone who knows him is aware of his faith in God. But they see it as a kind of escape hatch; there is nothing in his "religion" (as they call it) that would attract them to join him. They see nothing that, in their opinion, would add to their happiness, for a key factor is missing—the element of joy.

That reminds me of a neighbor who went calling for her church. In one home the response was, "No, thank you. We know some Christians, and if being a Christian is what makes them like they are—well, we're a lot happier than they appear to be."

In our defense I say that we are not generally aware of how we come across to the non-Christians around us. It is when they comment on the "vibrations" they pick up that our eyes are opened. I know this from an unforgettable experience.

Invited to speak to a women's gathering in Toronto, I chose the topic "Spring Housecleaning." I verbally cleaned out the drawers, cupboards, and closets of the "works of the flesh," then proceeded to refill them with the fruit of the Spirit (Galatians 5). I really labored the point of *joy,* crusading for happy faces as a testimony to what the Lord does in our lives. Because it was a Canadian audience—royalty oriented—I said, "Just as the Royal Standard flies over the palace when the queen is in residence, so joy is the flag that shows our King is in residence."

From the comments following the meeting, it appeared the women got the message. Toronto could expect an upsurge of joyful believers. Then a few of us went to a restaurant so that we might visit a little. The waitress took our order and started for the kitchen, then, turning, she faced me and said solicitously, "I think I'll bring your tea right away. You look as though you need something to pep you up." So much for me and my emphasis on letting joy show in our faces! To their credit let me say that not one of the women baited me about what the waitress had said.

I'll never know what that waitress saw in my face that afternoon, but I do know that it would have been futile for me at that moment to have told *her* anything about the joy of the Lord. I shall always remember her kindness in wanting to help "pep me up"; the greater favor she did for me, though, was to give me that glimpse of myself. Since then I have felt both a responsibility and a keen desire to "keep the flag flying," to demonstrate something of the abundant life Jesus offers.

This very special joy is no will-ó-the-wisp. Neither is it hard to come by. Peter calls it "joy unspeakable and full of glory" (1 Peter 1:8). But he had no "corner" on it. It is for us, too. "These things have I spoken unto you . . . that your joy might be full" (John 15:11), Jesus said. *Full*—not half, not partly full. And when we have it, why not show it? The other day I saw this graffiti on a wall: "If you have joy in your heart, please notify your face."

Before we let the joy shine out, we must *let it in*. We can curtain it out in the way we shut out sunshine when we do not want it in a room. It seems significant that when our Lord was preparing His disciples for the days ahead when nothing would ever be the same, He spoke of joy—His joy and "your joy," and He assured them, "Your joy no man taketh from you" (John 16:22). It cannot be taken from us by others. But I wonder if we rob ourselves of that deep joy.

37

THE JOY THAT COMES AFTERWARDS

Not every day will find us rejoicing outwardly. Sometimes God has to teach us lessons—chasten us—and that is not a joyful experience while it lasts. It is *"grievous,"* the Bible tells us (Hebrews 12:11). But that is not the end. There is an "afterwards" that promises joy. I confess that when I read that verse I used to stop at "the peaceable fruit of righteousness," not heeding what followed: *"unto them which are exercised thereby."* One day I recognized that not all of us are exercised by God's disciplining. Therefore not everyone reaps the reward. That can be likened to two children both of whom misbehave and are "chastened" by their father. Soon after, the one comes tearful and repentant to his dad, they make up, and the child is happy again. The other sulks, pouts, and gets angry. So, because he is not exercised by his father's chastening, he misses out on all the joy of reconciliation.

So it is with any believer. We can profit from chastening, and the joy is restored.

THE JOY THAT'S HARD TO LIVE WITH

Despite what we have already discussed, one kind of joy is hard to take: that is *unmitigated* joy. I have in mind the Christian who seems to be always one hundred percent on top, the one who "feels like singing all the time." I confess I am not in that category. So it was a good day for me when I learned that nobody—*nobody*—is emotionally on top *all the time.*

Why is this so?

Because we are human. David the psalmist knew a lot about joy. But he puzzled over his low feelings. *"Why art*

38

thou cast down, O my soul?" he questioned (Psalm 42:11; 43:5). David was able to come up with a solution to that temporary depression: "Hope thou in God." Nevertheless, he had his moments when joy was not uppermost.

We can identify with the psalmist. We are no less in God's hands when, just by virtue of our being part of the human race with all its pressures, life batters and nearly overwhelms us. We, too, can hope in God. Like a surfer caught in a wave, we can resurface; we do not have to drown.

If I sound as though I am contradicting my plea for the Christian to look joyful, such is not my intention. Rather, I am thinking of our being realistic, of not "being joyful" just to keep up appearances.

We are promised a deep joy *that remains.* That is not always an overt, bubbling-over experience. Sometimes such "joy" can be more properly labeled happiness—it is dependent upon what happens.

There are occasions when another Christian near us may be hurting. At such times, our unmitigated, obvious joyfulness might come across to the suffering person as a kind of mockery of his or her own situation and feelings. We need, then, to be sensitive as to overdoing our, "Rejoice in the Lord, brother!" or, "Where's your Christian *joy?"* The latter may cause a fellow Christian to question his spirituality. On the other hand, it may make him downright angry.

There is, without question, a constant joy that glows from the inside; it does not need to be proclaimed. I think of a neighbor, a woman who has been a believer for just three or four years. I can tell without her first saying a word that she is welling over with joy. Something shows in her eyes. "OK," I say, "tell me, and we'll rejoice together."

Jesus gives high priority to joy, and we can also.

It's good to keep in mind that the joy of the Lord is available to meet our need, whatever our temperament. That understanding will keep us from being critical or having a judgmental attitude toward a fellow Christian who does not demonstrate his joy in the way we do ourselves.

THE JOY THAT TRIUMPHS

Joy has in it the elements that make for endurance. It is the joy of crossing the finish line first that drives an athlete to keep on with his grueling workouts. The joy of accomplishment makes less tedious the musician's long hours of practice. The joy of seeing a book in print is a force that motivates the writer, making worthwhile the "burning of the midnight oil." Transcending all these is the experience of our Lord Jesus Christ, "who for the joy that was set before Him endured the cross" (Hebrews 12:2).

In the ensuing centuries martyrs have gone to their deaths with notable joy; history records that many of them sang praises to God even while the flames licked their doomed bodies. This century has had its own quota of Christian martyrs in a number of foreign lands, and stories are told of their joy under severe trial.

Not all trial means martyrdom or prison. Once when the Lord allowed me to go through a period of trauma, a friend —a fellow writer—said to me, "The best writing comes out of prison." I knew what he meant. He was not alluding to Paul in his Roman prison or to John Bunyan in the Bedford jail. There are other "prisons"; grief can and does imprison some people for the rest of their lives. Others break free, and (as my friend intimated) the world is better for the writing that comes out of their sad experiences. Such a man was the nineteenth-century Scottish preacher, George Matheson, who endured his own "prison." As a young man committed to the ministry, he was given the dire verdict that he was going blind. That was just the initial blow, for when his fiancée learned that he would soon be sightless, she broke the engagement. George Matheson might have let this double tragedy embitter and imprison him, and then doubtless we would never have heard of him. Somehow he was enabled not to let it blight his life, and out of the depths of his mingled faith and shattered hopes he gave us the hauntingly beautiful hymn "O Love That Wilt Not Let Me Go." Though we were not a Christian family, my mother sang hymns to us, and this hymn was one of her favorites, especially the verse that says:

> O Joy that seekest me through pain,
> I cannot close my heart to Thee;
> I trace the rainbow through the rain,
> And feel the promise is not vain
> That morn shall tearless be.

I have heard it said that when God sends tears into the Christian's eyes, it is so that He can show him a rainbow. If that is so, some people see the rainbow and recognize God's love and His promises of sunshine after rain; others do not.

I like what the late James Hunter, longtime editor of Canada's *Evangelical Christian* magazine said: "Who would not want to have tears when *God is going to wipe them away!*"

Meanwhile, under every circumstance and whatever our personality makeup, we can know what Nehemiah proved

41

to be true in his own day, "The joy of the LORD is your strength" (Nehemiah 8:10).

If the world ever needed to know some joy-filled people, it is now. Nothing will more impress the people we want to reach for Christ than our ability to be joyful under stress (for the most part, the unsaved realize *they* could not have such an attitude). It is when they come with their question, "How *can* you?" that we are in a good position to tell of our faith. Our triumph over trouble acts as a magnet to draw seeking persons toward us.

THE SOURCE OF LASTING JOY

Because we live in a materialistic society, most of us have been programmed to think that joy always goes hand in hand with prosperity (or at least the lack of calamity). But is that so? Or can we know joy in the midst of material disaster?

The prophet Habakkuk would teach us a helpful lesson along that line. See Habakkuk 3:17-18:

"Although the fig tree shall not blossom, neither shall fruit be in the vines; the labour of the olive shall fail, and the fields shall yield no meat; the flock shall be cut off from the fold, and there shall be no herd in the stalls . . ." Sound like the end of things? Economic disaster; end result, starvation.

What would be Habakkuk's reaction? Even though those dire things should happen, the prophet continued:

"Yet I will rejoice in the Lord, I will joy in the God of my salvation" (italics added). The prophet was saying, "God will not fail; my true source of joy will not be taken from me." And note the "I will." A joyful heart in the midst

42

of bleak circumstances calls for an act of the will, for it is generally all too easy at such times to think. *What do I have to be joyful about?*

The day is coming when, according to Psalm 16:11, we will know fullness of joy. In the meantime, we can know the joy of the Lord, and by His grace we can demonstrate it to other people. And don't think they do not notice. Let me provide another personal experience (to somewhat offset the earlier one).

On a recent Sunday morning between Sunday school and our second worship service, some friends and I were chatting over coffee on the church patio. One of the group, who had attended the earlier service, mentioned the topic of the pastor's sermon: "Joy." Then she remarked, "Jeanette won't have to go to that one."

My immediate response was, "I like that. I like it that you think so." Then I said a silent, "Thank You, Lord. You are so good to let me hear this, to let me know that *to some degree* those around me can see something of the joy you give me so abundantly."

Frequently, nothing will so validate our spoken beliefs as joy that shows on the outside.

It *is* possible to become a magnetic Christian, to know the plus of a joy-filled life.

4

A PACKET OF POSSIBILITIES:

The Plus of Good Expectations

Expectations come in two kinds: the good and the bad, or the positive and the negative.

Some people have a special ability to reject the negative as the only alternative. I am reminded of my daughter when she was a little girl. We lived in Canada, and in the summer almost every outdoor treat we planned had to include a "weather permitting" clause. One morning when we were all looking forward to a picnic, the weather forecaster came on the radio with his gloomy prediction, "Intermittent showers all day." *There goes our outing,* I thought. But not so my Jeannie. Quite unperturbed by the expert's prognosis, she kept on getting ready for the picnic. She totally dismissed the topic of the weather with an airy, "What does that man know? He hasn't even asked *Jesus."*

I have to admit that my daughter did not get her good-expectations attitude from me. For too many years I fitted better into the other category, which psychologists are now calling "catastrophic expectations." I was a bit of a crepe hanger. Let a telegram come to our home, and I immediately expected the worst. An official-looking letter had me conjuring up a tax audit or some equally intimidating experi-

45

ence. It did not matter that almost none of my catastrophic expectations had ever materialized (reason is not generally part of such thinking). Carried to its logical conclusion, however, such an attitude could eventually cause one to expect the worst from God—as though He were out to "get" us!

The very opposite attitude characterizes another person I know. With a merry twinkle in his eyes, he says, "I can hardly wait to get up in the morning to see what God is up to." Each day is a packet of good possibilities to that man. And as a business executive he has a tremendous influence on his colleagues and employees, for good expectations can be as contagious as poor ones.

Some of us, aware of our negative attitudes concerning what a day may bring, rationalize that they have to do with our temperament. "That's the type of person I *am*." The implication is: "I can't do anything about it." That kind of thinking may pass in the secular world, but Christians have the resources for change. In fact, Paul spells it out for us in 2 Corinthians 5:17: "When someone becomes a Christian he becomes a brand new person inside. He is not the same any more. A new life has begun!"* "All things are become new," the King James Version phrases it. *All* things. Would that not include getting rid of negative attitudes? We realize, of course, that some change will be gradual. Attitudes that have taken years to become a part of us (as when the convert is an adult), will not vanish instantaneously with the new birth.

How can we know when we are moving in the right direction? Sometimes the Lord graciously uses someone to en-

*The Living Bible.

46

courage us that a change is taking place. For instance, some time ago a friend greeted me and then said, "You seem to always expect good things to happen, Jeanette." Her eyes held both questioning and longing. I was glad that new attitude of mine was showing and inwardly thanked the Lord for His patience with me.

Have you thought that *expecting* good things means you can enjoy them even before they happen?

I should explain that I am not advocating the notion that we will go through life without trials or disappointments. Such an idea is contrary to the Scriptures. But we can live with a healthy outlook toward what the day will bring, rather than burdening ourselves with expectations that nothing will go right.

I mentioned "healthy outlook." How well I know that untold numbers of people in our society are far from being healthy, either physically or emotionally. It must be very difficult for them, many times, to have a bright attitude toward life. They merit our compassion, our prayer, and never our criticism. And we can all the more thank God for His goodness in giving us whole bodies and emotional stability, when that is the case.

WHY WE CAN HAVE GOOD EXPECTATIONS

It is not enough to have good *feelings*. Unless we have a solid basis for them, feelings may be fleeting or intermittent. So there has to be a rationale for good expectations.

Why do I expect good things from God? Because of who He *is*—because He is unchanging—because He knows my needs and promises to supply them—because His mercies are "new every morning" (Lamentations 3:22-23)—because I know Jesus Christ as my Savior, and He has promised to be with me always—because He has gone to prepare an eternal home for me—and a hundred other "becauses."

Why wouldn't I have happy expectations?

It is possible to be saved and still to go on for years living a minus kind of life. Yet the Lord is so willing to fill our days with pluses. As Annie Johnson Flint so beautifully expresses it:

> For out of His infinite riches in Jesus,
> He giveth and giveth and giveth again!

I am ashamed that it took me so long to appreciate all that is ours in Christ and to apply it practically in my daily life.

Now let me tell what has effected an ongoing change. I simply began to take the Bible at face value, take it and the Author of it *seriously*. From just memorizing Bible verses (and being a bit smug about how many I had learned), I began to internalize and personalize what they were saying.

Reading the Bible one day I saw as though for the first time four words in John 15:16: "I have chosen you." I blinked and read the verse again. Chosen by the Lord Jesus Christ! That is special—and who does not like to feel special? Later, I read in Ephesians 1:4 that I was part of God's long-range plan. I was *chosen before the foundation of the world,* that verse told me. Chosen *in Christ*. What security! God is not going to change His mind about a choice He made that long ago. That truth is a tremendous source of and reason for happy expectations.

Add to being chosen the fact that each child of God is *"accepted in the beloved"* (Ephesians 1:6). What a confi-

48

dence-inspiring, comforting truth that is. So many people around us have no such basis for feeling accepted—or chosen. They have little to cause them to feel special and that can influence their entire outlook on life. So it's good to have that in mind when we see a person who has negative attitudes. We will then have all the more motivation to relate to such people what the Lord is willing to do in their lives, how He will make them feel accepted, worthwhile, and special.

The next verse that contributed to building up my own good expectations was John 1:12: "As many as received him, to them gave he power to become the sons of God." That is the transaction that places us in God's family, members in full standing with all the rights and privileges it brings.

As if that were not enough, John further excites our imagination with, *"Now* are we the sons of God, and it doth not yet appear what *we shall be"* (1 John 3:2, italics added). We might try until the Lord comes and still not be able to visualize the glories that lie ahead of us. But we *can* expect everything to be in keeping with what we know about our heavenly Father and His Son, Jesus Christ. The mere anticipation can spark positive expectations.

Why then do some Christians go through life with a kind of hangdog posture? Children of the King, they tend to act and think of themselves as nobodies. They cannot seem to accept that they are purchased at a great price (not silver or gold *because there was not enough*); it took the shed blood of our Savior. Anyone who cost that much just has to be valuable; Jesus did not die for "nobodies." We are all His "somebodies." We are whole persons, "complete in Him" (Colossians 2:10).

I like what Pastor Wilbur Nelson once said on his "Morning Chapel Hour" broadcast: "Every person needs a plus in his life to make him complete—and the plus is Christ."

We can begin to reflect this plus of feeling worthwhile in our relationships with other people. We can reach out a hand with the good expectation that the other person will respond. Not everyone will, but with our changing attitude, we will not be crushed or feel rejected. The other person may need our reaching out toward him even though he cannot quite reciprocate. Everybody needs encouragement, and our good expectations of others can often provide people with such encouragement.

What are you expecting God to do for you today?

I would emphasize *today* because it is here; today is with us. It is both good and healthy to look forward to an enjoyable tomorrow, but not at the expense of today. Some people I meet seem to believe they had better be careful with their happiness, their peace, their joy, and guard it well, as though it might get away from them. Others appear to fear that if they appropriate a lot of those good things today, there will not be enough for tomorrow. They have an "it's too good to last" outlook. Would that not be at least partially because of lack of faith in God's ability to provide without measure for His children?

There is sufficient evidence in the Bible to convince us that God has a never-ending supply. His bank is never going to fail; and I believe that He delights in having us cash our Philippians 4:19 checks.

God is not limited to our expectations. Sometimes, when

I have needed a particular thing, as I have prayed I have reminded the Lord of a source He has tapped on other occasions to supply a similar need. But time and again, God has used other means than I had felt sure He would use. In the early days of our ministry, life was largely a faith venture. Where we were serving as home missionaries, money was scarce. Yet I look back on those days with nothing but joyful memories. Every day was an adventure in faith, and a trip to the post office was sheer excitement. In some instances, it was years before we met some of the people whose hearts God had moved to meet our needs. Our expectations were consistently high, and God just as consistently met them. Not only did that encourage us, but it also blessed our congregation, for we were quick to tell what God had done. That, in turn, caused many of the congregation to have good expectations.

A good measure of faith is in expectation. Because faith is not of ourselves, "it is the gift of God" (Ephesians 2:8), then expectation—good expectation—is a gift of God.

The only way to enjoy a gift is to accept it.

Sometimes I have asked the Lord if it would be all right with Him if I reason, "According to my *expectations* (in addition to faith) be it unto me."

THE REASONABLENESS OF GOOD EXPECTATIONS

I have pondered at times how Christians can profess to believe that "all things work together for good," yet have negative expectations. Who makes things work for our good? *God.* Is He also busy making things work together for evil? Of course not. I like what my brother, a minister, says on the subject of Romans 8:28: *"Things* do not work for

51

good; God works in the 'things' [circumstances]." I often liken the process to baking. Suppose you collect all the ingredients for a cake: flour, baking powder, baking soda, salt, sugar, eggs, flavoring, and whatever else the recipe calls for. You set these on the table and call the family for dessert. Can you picture their reaction? Now take the same "things," mix them together, let them "work together" for the prescribed time in the recommended heat. *Then* put your product on the kitchen table. You will not even have to call the family!

So it is with our circumstances when we are God's children. We can trust Him to work out the "things" for our good. Why then should we not have good expectations?

5

BUT 490 TIMES:

The Plus of a Forgiving Spirit

Forgiveness: one of the greatest themes in all the Bible—and one I like to dwell on.

For the past few years I have spoken to many groups in the States, in Canada, and overseas. Those opportunities have included women's retreats and conferences, Christian women's clubs, and other functions, secular among them.

Without fail, the subject of forgiveness has evoked intense interest and some reaction. "How can I *ever* forgive?" The question has come to me with rebellious head-tossing and also with tears.

Of the wealth that is mine as a Christian, the most cleansing and liberating gem is what happens when by God's grace I can have a forgiving spirit.

It is not always easy.

How well I remember the day that I saw forgiveness in a new light. My reading that morning had included the Lord's Prayer, and, as we tend to do, I had mentally skipped over that familiar part of Matthew 6. Then I was struck with what came to me from Jesus' adding a postscript to that pattern prayer. The prayer, encompassing verses 9 through 13*a,* uses fifty-two words (KJV). Then, as though underscoring a primary emphasis, the Lord Jesus added twenty-nine words on the subject *forgiveness.* "For if we forgive men their trespasses, your heavenly Father will also forgive you; But if ye forgive not men their trespasses, neither will your Father forgive your trespasses" (Matthew 6:14-15).

Surely He must have meant us to give particular heed to that teaching.

That was not the first time Jesus had emphasized the importance of right relationships with other people as a prerequisite to right relationship with God and acceptance with Him when we come to Him in prayer (see Matthew 5:23-24). Mark likewise mentions the correlation of prayer and forgiveness (11:25-26).

I like it that Jesus expects the best of us. He deals first with the positive, and only then does He move into the results of a negative response to His teaching. And note the personal pronoun *you.* Forgiveness is a do-it-yourself project; no one can do your forgiving for you.

What happens when we do not forgive? We are in a sense chained to the one whom we "cannot" forgive.

It may not make sense to us that we should be expected to forgive every wrong and the person who wrongs us. I can recall times when I said to God, "Even *You* wouldn't require this of me, Lord." But I was wrong; in such thinking I was in essence making up my own rules. Well did Jesus know we would never be free of the person whom we do not forgive, and that such a one would haunt our prayer lives.

We will find as we seek to have communion with our Lord that the ones we "cannot forgive" will invade our minds, distracting us and detracting from any and all joy in the

Lord. It will be as if a thick veil hid God from our view (see Isaiah 59:2).

Jesus painted a word picture of a man bringing his gift to the altar, then being reminded (by conscience? by the Holy Spirit?) that he had something against his brother. At that point there was just one thing to do: forget the offering and do something about the strained relationship with the brother. The Lord would still be there when the worshiper returned. He was not rejecting either the gift or the giver. God, who made us, knows we can go through all the motions of worship, yet still carry a devastating, unforgiving spirit. So it is for our own well-being that He instructs us to forgive. He is not standing by the scales balancing off how much we forgive, so that His forgiveness of us will measure just that much, ounce for ounce. No, He loves us enough to want the best for us, and we are so constituted that an unforgiving attitude is an enemy of all tranquility of the spirit.

Not only is it spiritually healthy for us to get rid of an unforgiving spirit, but it is also emotionally healthy. Psychologists, psychiatrists, and other counselors are besieged by clients, many of whom are suffering from unresolved guilt feelings. The prescription *forgive* would ease a multitude of such problems. Not only so, for in our day experts accept the view that the body and the mind are so correlated that they "catch each other's diseases." Thus the healing balm of a forgiving spirit can affect our physical well-being.

The Lord knew all about that when He issued His strong decree as to the place of forgiveness in our lives. It applies both to Christian and non-Christian, but the burden is on the believer because God promises us the grace needed to handle the problem.

When the exhortation to forgive is taken seriously and acted upon, beautiful things happen. I recall such an instance. We were holding an evangelistic campaign in our church, and the preacher had been dealing with the matter of forgiveness. Following the service a woman, a rather new Christian, came to my husband and said, "Pastor, I have a brother I haven't spoken to for years. He lives about fifty miles from here. Tomorrow I'm going to take the day off from work and go to see him. Will you and Mrs. Lockerbie come with me, Pastor?" We gladly agreed to go.

Here was a Christian who had been stirred to new dedication but who had been "stopped at the altar" by the remembrance that things were not right between her and her brother. She humbled herself to admit her part in the problem. She inconvenienced herself to physically bridge the distance between them. And God did the rest. The rift was mended, the relationship restored.

Not that day but later, the brother sought his own forgiveness from God and accepted Christ as his Savior.

Not always will the result be so rewarding. It may be you are asking, What if the other will not do his part in forgiving when I go more than halfway? That happens. We would not be realistic if we expected that God's ideal is always experienced when we seek to follow His teaching.

I have been saddened many times as I have thought of a dear friend. At one time another Christian treated him wrongly and, for all the years since, that friend has been bitter, vengeful and unforgiving. The sad part is that he has hurt both himself and his family by his attitude. God has blessed the other person, who long ago asked for forgiveness (and received it from God but not from his Christian brother when he sought him out and begged for forgiveness).

Believe me, that is hard to take. I know, for I too have tried to effect a reconciliation by seeking forgiveness, only to be refused.

It is not always easy to leave the consequences to the Lord; but that is the scriptural way and the best way in the end. The matter is in God's hands. We have obeyed His instructions and offered and sought forgiveness. We cannot do the Holy Spirit's work. Meantime, our prayers are not hindered as formerly when we held a grudge. (A psychologist has defined a grudge as "hostility sitting on a shelf waiting to be taken down.") Until such grudge feelings are destroyed through forgiveness, they will be a perpetual potential for worse relationships.

"But," we may say, "Why should *I* be the one to take the first step to make the gesture of forgiveness? After all—" And we justify ourselves.

Why, indeed? One, we receive God's blessing; two, we materially aid our own well-being, for an unforgiving spirit is self-destructive; three, we assist the other person, who may just be waiting for the slightest sign that forgiveness is available and forthcoming.

Forgiveness is a prerequisite to genuine and continuing love. A pastor I know has through the years offered as a life verse to the couples he has married, "Be ye kind one to another, tenderhearted, forgiving one another, even as God for Christ's sake hath forgiven you" (Ephesians 4:32). He tells of their incredulous looks. "Forgive each other! Who, us?" they seem to say. "What will *we* ever have to forgive?" But the day comes when they realize that a forgiving spirit is one of the most needful ingredients in marriage.

God's "beautiful people" are those who are forgiving. Why shouldn't we be, with such a pattern of forgiveness in Christ our Savior?

Dr. Raymond Ortlund has said, "From the cross Jesus did not appeal, 'Father, *love* them'; but rather, 'Father, *forgive* them.' "

"But I get *tired* of forgiving some people," I have heard a few Christians say.

Peter did, too. And his complaint and Christ's handling of it provide an unforgettable lesson and a glimpse of the Jesus who could use satire to make His point.

Seven times would have stretched Peter's forgiving spirit to its limits. But Jesus, in the way He has of multiplying in order to bless us, exhorted His impetuous disciple to think *seventy times seven*. Can you imagine Peter saying with mingled amazement and resistance to the idea, "But 490 times, Lord!"

In my opinion that is where the satire comes in; Christ gave a precise, measurable boundary for forgiveness.

We can picture the scene. The disciples may have had a bad day among themselves, and mending fences had meant saying, "I'm sorry," and, "Please forgive me," a number of times. But Peter (whose conduct the Scripture honestly portrays with so many lessons for us) had apparently "had it"; he was going to settle that matter of where his obligation to forgive began—and especially where it ended.

Had Jesus meant 490 times literally, what kind of obligation would that place on us (or on Peter, for that matter)?

Sometimes in a meeting I work that out on a chalkboard. Here, let us just imagine a miniature chart. It will require 490 spaces for checking off.

The day comes when someone sins against me or offends me in some manner. Being a magnanimous, forgiving person, I say, "I forgive you," and I go and record the forgiveness on my chart. (Remember, that would mean having a chart for everyone who might possibly need my forgiveness.)

Sadly, a similar incident occurs—but fortunately the person still has 489 chances left. I go to check off forgiveness number two, but the pencil freezes in my hand. I cannot do it.

Why? Why can I not carry through that accounting process? Did not Jesus say 490 times, and how can I obey without keeping track?

I cannot make the second check mark because the first is still there, shouting at me, *"You did not forgive* the first time!"

What, then, was Jesus really teaching Peter (and you and me)?

"We don't keep score, Peter. We forgive—and forgive—and forgive."

What if God kept score on us? What if He had a chart indicating that "this many times *and no more* will I forgive you"? How many of us would long ago have used up our quota? But I read in my Bible that He forgives *all* our iniquities (Psalm 103:3). I read, "I, even I, am he that blotteth out thy transgressions . . . and will not remember thy sins" (Isaiah 43:25). Blots out? That leaves no place for a recording chart with 490 squares. Nor does it allow for "burying the hatchet, but keeping the handle sticking up." God does not keep handy our sin that He has forgiven in

59

order to throw it in our faces the next time we come pleading His forgiveness. *We* do this, and it devastates the one who had believed we had truly forgiven. But God does not do this to us.

How Can I Forget?

"I can forgive, but I just *cannot* forget." How often a woman has said that to me after I have spoken on the subject of a forgiving spirit. Usually she speaks those words not in anger or bitterness but almost wistfully—as if she would love to be able to forget as well as forgive.

Yes, it is hard to forget. But it is possible to *remember without bad feelings.* The incident is still real in our minds, but the anger, humiliation, or whatever other negative emotion was part of it, fades. Not all at once, but it does. So it may be that whereas for God, forgiveness is instantaneous because He *is* God, for us humans forgiveness may be a process. One thing I am quite sure of is that we must *will* to forgive. Jesus made that clear in that postscript I mentioned earlier. Our feet will never take us to seek forgiveness from someone until our mind has signaled to our brain that *we will* to do this. (Perhaps that is part of loving the Lord our God with our minds.)

A "How To" suggestion: Because we are all different—we act and react differently to similar situations—I can only recount what God has shown me. Having taken the scriptural steps toward accepting my own share of responsibility, then asking the other person to forgive me, I try not to dwell on the matter. When destructive thoughts invade my mind in spite of myself, I ask the Lord to help me not let something that is past spoil what He has for me that day. God delights

60

to help us grow. Along the way He has surprised me with so many good things and exciting experiences that I would be not only an ingrate but a fool to permit the weeds of unforgiveness to flourish in the garden of my mind.

One proved method to rid ourselves of such weeds is to pray earnestly for the other person or people. Ask God to bless them as much as He blesses us. It works!

Ultimately, the true motivation for having a forgiving spirit is that having been forgiven much, we can love much. God has poured out His forgiveness *without measure*—to the sacrificing of His Son for our sins. With so much forgiveness available for us, we can afford to be generous in forgiving other people.

AND FORGIVE YOURSELF

It is a paradox that we who can accept forgiveness from God cannot forgive ourselves. I hear this all the time: "I just can't forgive myself." The person usually goes on to assure me, "Oh, I know *God* has forgiven me," and he may quote 1 John 1:9.

I cannot quite go along with the man who wrote, "Forgive yourself little and others much," however well he meant that.

If I cannot forgive myself, I cannot accept God's forgiveness. How then am I going to feel forgiven? And am I not in a sense refuting verses I know and quote, such as, "Therefore being justified by faith, we have peace with God through our Lord Jesus Christ" (Romans 5:1), and "There is therefore now no condemnation to them which are in Christ Jesus" (Romans 8:1)?

Why should you or I go through life partially paralyzed

61

spiritually, all because of having an unforgiving spirit toward someone (including, perhaps, ourselves)?

Developing a forgiving spirit takes time. But it can be done. It is wise to keep in mind that likely we will not all be "instant forgivers."

I am reminded of a conversation I heard between a POW home from North Vietnam, and Corrie ten Boom. Corrie had just been introduced to the United States Navy officer, and she asked him, "Have you *forgiven* the North Vietnamese, Commander?"

His reply, after some seconds, was, "It will take time, ma'am; it will take time."

I could not help appreciating that realistic answer. It promised more deep and lasting forgiveness than if the POW had given quick assent. The wound was deep; it would take time to heal.

However long it may take some of us, we can ultimately and, with God's help, truly forgive.

An unforgiving spirit will always be a minus in our lives. A forgiving spirit is a plus.

6

YOU CAN'T GO IT ALONE:

The Plus of Being Both a Giver and a Receiver

"No man is an island, intire of it self," John Donne philosophized from his sixteenth-century vantage point. He was but restating what Paul the apostle had declared to the Roman Christians of his day: "None of us liveth to himself, and no man dieth to himself" (Romans 14:7).

Almost anyone would give mental assent to the concept of human interdependence. Yet there are those who have the attitude *"I would rather do it myself."* Those go-it-aloneers seem to be emotionally incapable of admitting to having limitations. I am not one of them. It is never a problem to me to admit, "I can't do this or that," and help is generally forthcoming, for we are born with a need to give as well as to take.

One day on a plane trip, with time to ponder, I toyed with the thought of how kind other people are to me, almost without exception. They are ready with their help, even while they tease me for my ineptness (locking my car with the keys inside, and so on). With the banter there is also noticeable warmth and a smile. *Why?* I asked myself as the plane droned on.

To my surprise, the same topic surfaced later in the day

as I was with a group of missionary friends. One man said of a colleague, "She just has to be the most *un*mechanically-minded person in the whole world!" But he was saying it with that same warmth in his voice and with a smile.

"Other women could learn from her," the missionary continued. Turning to me, he said, "Jeanette, in your travels you must run into some snags. You should take a leaf out of this gal's book on how to get people to help you—and *like doing it.*"

Inwardly chuckling, I thanked him even as I thought, *What made him single out one woman colleague as an example? Surely there must be others equally in need of help, others who are faced with situations they are not very able to handle but which would be simple for most missionary men.*

Actually it did not take too much probing to find at least a partial explanation for the willing male cooperation. For one thing, obviously the man was *allowed to help.* His offer was neither shrugged off nor openly rejected. Add to that the apparent ego satisfaction a man gets from being a help to someone who needs it. (As the conversation proceeded I gathered that the "helpless" woman missionary was very much respected for her contribution in her own area of expertise. Nevertheless she could accept her limitations; she was willing to admit it when she needed help, not insisting, "I can do it myself," and floundering.) Such a person does not need the satisfaction of never having to say, "I can't do it myself."

Second, that woman was able to *let a man be a man,* without feeling inferior herself. Such an attitude engenders good feelings in the man. In turn he tends to have good feelings toward women.

As a contrast to that example, other women appear to have to be proving something all the time. They seemingly cannot tolerate accepting help from the opposite sex. An instance comes to mind. With a few friends I was fellowshiping in a home, and at one point a young woman in the group excused herself and rose to leave, gathering up her things as she did so. Both hands were full, and when she stepped toward the door, one of the men walked over to open it for her. Almost rudely she elbowed him away and said, "I can open the door myself." The look on the man's face revealed something of what that woman's behavior had caused him to feel. That is just one example. No doubt you have seen many others.

If we are honest we will admit that we all need someone's help at one time or another. In the home there are certainly some things a man can do better than most women. But the husband does not always get the opportunity to do them. Capable or not, the wife just has to "do it herself." (I know we are on touchy ground here; some women would wait a lifetime for a job around the house to be done if they did not undertake it themselves. But the other side is to be considered. The man must be allowed to be the man and to exercise his desire to help.)

Perhaps my years as a pastor's wife have contributed to my attitudes toward accepting help when it is offered. I have always tended to back away from the superefficient, able-to-do-everything woman in the congregation, at times viewing such a person as something of a menace. But again, there is the matter of balance. *Without* such church members some things might never get done that need to be done.

WHO WOULD THE HELPER HELP?

One of the somewhat unsung gifts that the Lord gave to His church is the gift of "helps" (1 Corinthians 12:28).

Obviously, then, God has ordained that some Christians would have the special ministry of being a helper. We all know such people. Frequently we say of them, "They're never in the spotlight, but what would our church be without them?" or, "She doesn't say much, but she's always around when someone needs a helping hand."

But what if nobody would accept the offered help? Whom would the helper help? How could he administer the gift God has given him? Where would it fit in?

Have you ever thought that in being willing to *take* help we may even have a ministry? (That is a comforting thought to people like me who do need a lot of help if we are to function at our best for God.)

BEWARE OVERDEPENDENCY

There is a difference between being able to take help and being a total leaner. So let me make clear that in no way am I advocating dependency for its own sake. We need not go through life with a perennial little-girl attitude. An always-dependent trait creates its own problems, for people are quick to see it as a pose, sometimes as a bid for attention. Although help may be given, it will frequently be accompanied by a feeling of resentment toward the one it is given to. The helper may believe he is being manipulated and may develop feelings of hostility toward the person. No one likes to think he is being used. Psychologist Haim Ginott wrote, *"Things* are for using, people are for loving."

Overdependence is generally a mark of the immature person.

However, it is possible to be quite mature and yet not be good at doing certain things. In the areas of our incompetency we must learn to accept help graciously without in any degree supposing that it is our due.

One of my greatest inadequacies is in the area of finding my way. I have genuinely tried to develop that sense of direction so many others have, but I do not improve. Even with precise directions, I often have difficulties, so much so that when setting out to speak at a meeting I regularly allow time to get lost. One rainy Saturday evening I was having problems finding the right turns. After going in circles I came to an unmarked crossroad, and I can still recall sitting there wailing, "Lord, I just don't know how to find the place I'm going to—and now I don't even know my way *home.*" Suffice it to say that God heard that desperate prayer and sent help along. My own difficulty does give me understanding of others who have the same problem.

Everybody has some area of incompetency. So may I suggest that whatever yours is, do not let it put you into a "can't do anything by myself" straitjacket. The tendency may be present to not even try. It is easier to stay home, for instance, than to venture out and get lost. Also, well-meaning friends sometimes would protect us by saying, "It'll be too much for you." Thank them for their consideration but do not let their suggestion be a stop sign. If God is opening a new door for you, think at least twice before being intimidated by any hazards it seems to present. When it is indeed God's venture for you, He will give corresponding peace to *you,* not necessarily to those who care for your interests.

WHO DOESN'T NEED HELP?

Again, from the truly helpless infant to the most vigorous and seemingly self-sufficient adult, at some point everyone has to depend on others. The dependence may be upon the other person's skills, his strength, his experience, or his money. But "no man is an island."

In reminding us of our interdependence, Paul was speaking practical truth; moreover he was likely speaking from his own experience. We tend to think of the first-century Christians—and Paul in particular—as being unusually able to cope. Nothing was too much for him to handle. Yet it was Paul who wrote, "I can do all things," and added, "through Christ which strengtheneth me" (Philippians 4:13). And, like us, Paul knew that God for the most part uses people to strengthen us. Think of some of Paul's experiences. How far would he have gotten in his over-the-wall-in-a-basket escape without human aid? Even before that, God sent Ananias to help Paul in his blind state; others washed and tended his lash-wounded back; the islanders on Malta warmed and fed Paul after his shipwreck. The sixteenth chapter of Romans is a veritable roll call of the people who helped Paul, his true yokefellows, as he called them (Philippians 4:3). Admirably aware that no one lives unto himself or by his own efforts entirely, Paul had the emotional capacity to accept help when he needed it. From his example and others, we see that not only does it make sense to accept help, but it is also scriptural.

It is difficult to imagine why some people are so insensitive as to not realize and recognize our interdependence.

Perhaps you have listened to someone describe his exploits for God. They have been amazing and apparently true. But have you wondered, *How did one man manage to do all that without some help? For there was not even one mention of any yokefellow.* Yet all human experience bears out the fact that no man or woman can exist and achieve totally unaided. Moses had his Aaron; David had his "mighty men." The gift of helps has played a major part throughout history. But it could not have done so if there had been none who would accept the help.

It might be well for you and me to pause right now and ask ourselves, *How many persons have helped me today, and in how many ways? How much would have been left undone if I had insisted on not accepting help from anyone else?*

Then, turn the question around. Ask, *How many people have I helped today? in what ways and to what degree?*

I have noticed a special quality in many who have the gift of helps. They are *there* and are quick to anticipate another's needs. What strikes me so often is that they do not have to be specially noticed and praised to be kept happy. For the God-ordained helper, the doing of things for other people appears to be its own reward. At the same time they are usually most responsible, not neglecting their own duties on the pretext of being needed elsewhere. (Mr. or Mrs. Available, on the other hand, will leave their responsibilities at the mere suggestion that they might be needed in another place. In the process they continually frustrate the members of their own team, who should be able to depend on them.)

Complex beings, we do not always know why we do what we do. It is a good exercise, then, to deliberately question our attitudes and motives. As Socrates would teach us, "The unexamined life is not worth living." I try to keep this in mind and periodically look at my inabilities as well as my

69

abilities and what I am doing with them. I have asked myself a number of times, *Do I actually need people to help me, or am I (consciously or not) appearing to be "helpless" for my own ends?*

Other valid questions for the person who senses his possible overdependence are these: How willing am I to admit I need help? Will my asking for assistance cause me to feel inferior? How secure am I inwardly, and how does that affect my willingness to allow people to do me a favor or meet a need?

Similarly the *in*dependent would do well to assess their own dynamics. They might ask, What makes it so difficult for me to accept help? What ego satisfaction do I gain by my insistence on "doing it myself"? To what extent would accepting help lower my self-esteem?

As we probe our attitudes and feelings by asking honest, hard questions of ourselves, we may become willing to dip our flag of independence at times and not always have to say, "I'd rather do it myself."

Ultimately, whatever our makeup, we are driven to the true source. Like David, we learn that our help cometh from the Lord. And we cannot keep Him from helping us.

We drop a minus into our lives when we insist on being totally independent, for God has made us with a need to cooperate with other human beings. The plus comes when we act upon that fact.

7

YOU *CAN* DO SOMETHING WELL:

The Plus of Achievement

How often have you heard someone say, "I'm really not good at anything, so why should I try?"

In the last chapter we dealt with what some of us cannot do (or cannot readily do). We need to move now into the area of what we can do.

First, let us establish in our own minds that there *are* some things—at least one—that we each can do and do well. As I meet groups of women at retreats, Christian women's clubs, or other functions at which I speak, inevitably someone will say, "Oh, you don't know me, or you would realize I have no talents. I must have been behind the door when they were given out," or some such rationalization.

Not so.

God created us, and I cannot imagine the God of creation forming *any of us* to be useless. Moreover the Bible makes clear that each one has some gift. First Corinthians 12:4 speaks of diversities of gifts. In Romans 12:6 the implication is clear: *"Having then gifts,"* let us use them. The parable of the talents likewise teaches the fact of Christ's investment in His own servants and our accountability for our stewardship of what He has entrusted to us.

What keeps Christians living on a low level of effort?

One reason would appear to be that they have unrealistic ideas of achievement. That is understandable in the light of the glorification of Christian "stars" (many of them humble followers of Christ, but whose profession, success, or both puts them in the public eye). I have heard it said in snide fashion that the new trinity is Art, Athletics, and Entertainment. Whether or not, many from those and other areas of life are making names for themselves, and when they are avowed believers, other Christians elevate them to great heights. Consequently the tendency is for some who see themselves as lesser lights to settle for doing little. "Who am *I*, and what can *I* contribute?" appears to keep them on a low level of expectation of themselves and their abilities. All the while they are looking at other people and what they are accomplishing.

Frequently, people say, "I can't do what you do." At which point I do my best to draw them into conversation about their own interests. At the same time I am quick to assure them that I am not a many-talented person. I recall once being introduced to a group of ministers' wives and having the person introducing me wax rather extravagant, as sometimes happens on such occasions. Feeling uncomfortable, I cut short the introduction by suggesting the women might be interested in what I *cannot* do. "For instance, in the arts and crafts department where so many pastors' wives appear to be very creative, I'm a washout," I admitted.

"Do you mean," my introducer questioned, "that you couldn't teach any of your church women how to do these things?"

72

"Worse than that," I explained, "they couldn't teach me!" Even so, I am not without at least one talent. Nor are you. And God, who is just, will not require a five-talent return from His one- or two-talent investment in us.

RECOGNIZING YOUR TALENT

A prime reason why some men and women never gain the satisfaction and fulfillment that others enjoy is this: they have never made an effort to single out what *is* their God-given talent(s). And do not be unhappy if you find you have just one, for does that not narrow the field so that you can concentrate on that talent? Your one area of ability can make you a valuable specialist. By contrast, the many talented, not sure in which direction they can best succeed, can become victims of their seeming good fortune. Sometimes that results in a "buckshot approach": aiming at everything, hitting nothing. Or, it can mean that, with multiple options, the individual may hop from one thing to another, finding little success or sense of fulfillment (that need not be so, however).

So do not deplore your one talent. Make the most of it, rather than settling for, "I can't do much, so why try anything?"

"But how do I find out where my talent lies?" you may be questioning.

Let me assure you that you do not have to be a vocational guidance counselor in order to spot certain signs of ability. Here is an almost foolproof test you can give yourself. Close your eyes. Try to put your mind in neutral for a few moments. Then ask yourself this question: *If nothing stood in my way—not health, or finances, or obligations to others, or*

73

the expectations of others for me—if nothing *prevented me, what would I most like to do with the rest of my life?*

Really dwell on that; think about what you have dreamed of doing even though it has seemed an impossibility. You are very likely to discover that the thing *you dream of doing* is the very thing *you can do best.* And it is not impossible. God has not gifted you with a talent to then mock you by not letting you ever achieve in that direction. God does not will that you should be a victim of an impossible dream. More than likely, once you let yourself dwell on your abilities, it will become plain to you that you *do* have success experiences in a certain area.

Everyone needs to have success experiences in order to feel worthwhile. It is understandable that we will do best the thing in which we feel competent. Dr. Clyde Narramore says, "Your natural abilities are God's suggestions for your lifework." I strongly believe that. So it pays to ferret out that God-given talent. Then do not stop at dreaming about it. Turn your dreams into goals.

To illustrate, I cannot remember a time when I did not look up to writers; the attitude almost amounted to reverence. I could not think of anything in the world I would rather do than write, even though I had no reason to hope I would ever *be* a writer. Conversely, I never spent time dreaming, hoping, or wishing along lines in which I had no natural bent.

To sum up, the areas in which you have the greatest built-in interest are normally those for which you have natural ability and the capacity to achieve. That is a direct route to living on the plus side.

AGE HAS LITTLE TO DO WITH IT

Frequently I hear people say, "If I had only known sooner (about some ability) I might have gotten into that field." I understand what they are saying. But in a sense does not such thinking limit God's plan for them by confining it to a certain slot of time in their lives?

To be sure, the earlier we discover our talent(s) and seek to train in that direction, the more years we will have to be productive in that area. However, circumstances do not always permit us to take that course. When that is so, one of two things usually happens:

1. The person becomes somewhat sour, out of frustration. It is known that ability without training creates frustration. That frustration may be exhibited also in criticism. When a person has certain natural ability—say in art or music—without the necessary training, it is easy to criticize the person who is accomplishing what he is not. The negative feelings are reflected in the person's unhappiness with life.

2. The other option, when we cannot immediately proceed with our recognized area of ability, is to guard the dream until it *is* possible to do something about activating it. Meanwhile we do not have to be unhappy with ourselves and other people. God's will may well have a time-release factor. We have His promise that if we will delight ourselves in Him, He will give us the desires of our hearts (Psalm 37:4). It may be that God will grant some desires later in life, but the experience will be none the less delightful.

I was among "the writers who emerge over forty" that I keep reading about. God could have moved me into a writing ministry/career earlier. But He knows what is best for

75

us. He did not let me write until I had something to write about: a knowledge of His Word and His working in my life, much interaction with people as a minister's wife, opportunities for travel, and all that comes from much reading of good authors.

A few weeks ago I was complimenting a church organist, and this is what she told me: "I was always interested in music. But I was married and had a family before I realized I could be good at it." Her face was shining as she told me of the joy of having that new dimension in her life.

I am persuaded that the Lord has His ways of bringing us to the place of fulfillment, when we really want His will in our lives.

I live with the unshakable conviction that God *does* have a plan for our lives. Why wouldn't he? He has a plan for everything He created, and we are His *highest* creation. Ephesians 2:10 is clear on that: "We are His workmanship, created in Christ Jesus unto good works, which God hath before ordained."

For some, God's plan may be a steady ongoing course that provides daily peace and assurance that they are in His will. To others there come highlight experiences akin to Stop and Go signals, which guide them on God's path for them.

The outworking of God's plan in my own life, especially the past ten to fifteen years, has been exciting. At each new step it has been a matter of my being in the *right place* at the *right time* with the *right people* and the *right circumstances*. You might say, "Oh, well, that can just happen." Yes, it can, once or twice, and be coincidence. But only God can *consistently* set up such situations. The result of believing that is that I look into such seeming coincidences for God's hand and His purpose.

One of the joys of working with Dr. Ralph Byron on the book *Surgeon of Hope* was that his life, too, has been marked by such specific incidents. God would have him in a place *just once* (a seemingly almost impossible coincidence) with certain medical or military dignitaries. And time and again that was the key factor in advancing him toward God's ultimate area of service for him: Chief of Surgery at Duarte, California's world-famed City of Hope. For twenty-five years he has had fantastic experiences in serving his fellowmen and in consistently witnessing to his faith in Jesus Christ.

It was stimulating to me to find another who can precisely pinpoint situations that only God could have set up, and which then became clearer than road signs. In fact my involvement with Dr. Byron as his coauthor grew out of that thing we have in common. To quote him: "Jeanette believed that the incredible things God has ploughed into my life *could* happen."

So it pays to let God *be* God in your life; let Him lead you. But I suggest that you be eagerly on the outlook for His leading. God is more willing for us to achieve our potential than we are.

In that area of achievement we need to have a proper understanding of what achievement really is. Not all are called to visible, measurable success. Some of the greatest achievers I know are the *praying* people, those who take this ministry seriously—and they are all too few. I recall a woman in one of our congregations. We used to say of her, "Don't ask her to pray for something unless you really want it."

I have known of remarkable answers to her prayers. She was a simple, hardworking lady, but when she said, "I'll be praying," we could count on her to do so. Apparently she had discovered that was her God-given talent.

Such believers do not see themselves as relegated to a "lesser ministry" because they are less "active." Nor do they, generally, have an apologetic attitude ("all I can do is pray"). There will never be enough in that corps. And age has little to do with it.

THE PART OTHERS PLAY

We never know when something we say will influence another person. Although it is unmistakable that God uses His Word to speak to us and to direct us, He also uses people. In fact I have the proved conviction that we can best reach our potential when we are prodded by someone who cares for us and expresses that caring.

At one point in my life my husband was traveling in evangelism much of the time, our son and daughter were away in college, and I had few responsibilities. I recall the day I received a letter from Bruce saying, "Now that you don't have Jeannie and me and all our friends around the house, and with Dad away at times, you must have a hole in your life. Why don't you try professional writing? *I know you can do it.*"

With such confidence-inspiring encouragement, I began to believe *I could do it.*

My daughter, too, bless her, is a great motivator. How often a unique opportunity for service has come my way because Jeannie has suggested to someone who was in search of help in writing, "My mother will help you." Ultimately such a suggestion was what sparked my overseas ministry.

Encouraging and motivating the people around us: that is something worthwhile that we all can do. Nothing helps to create *self*-confidence more than knowing that those you care for, those whose opinion you respect, believe you have potential. Their confidence is contagious. But it has to be *expressed,* or how would we know they think we *can* do it?

THE ROUND PEG IN THE SQUARE HOLE

Have you sometimes wondered why certain people seem to be misfits?

Not always is that the result of failing to recognize where their abilities lie. Some people *despise* the talent God has given them; they prefer a vocation or profession they view as "better."

A businessman was noted for his faithful support of missionaries. I have been present when his unexpected gift was an answer to special prayer. But he was not satisfied to have that ministry. He stepped into pastoral work and from that time on never knew the gratification of a job well done. He had despised his "gift of helps," and came to know only failure.

Another man had been blessed with great talent for working with children. He could hold a large audience of boys and girls spellbound. Children loved him and crowded around him. Churches clamored for his ministry, for always there was a harvest of child conversions. Yet that Christian sought a "more important" sphere of service. For years he jumped in and out of various types of missionary work (having studied and been ordained to the ministry). But in nothing

79

else did he know the success he had enjoyed when working with children.

I have not related those instances to pinpoint the relative merits of one kind of Christian work or another. What I am emphasizing is that we will always do best and know the greatest blessing and fulfillment when we are utilizing the talent with which God has been pleased to endow us. Moreover, that is the talent for which we will have to give an account one day.

THE GOING-TO PEOPLE

Sometimes not lack of ability but sheer procrastination keeps people from achieving. I think of a missionary film titled *The Going To Family.** The film portrays Christians who really loved the Lord and desired to serve Him. They responded to the call of missions. But they stopped there. They never got past "going to" do something about it. They made a commitment, then let procrastination rob them of the fulfillment of achieving something significant for God.

I hear people in their twenties and thirties say, "I believe I know what God wants me to do with my life, and sometime I'm going to do something about it." Predictably, some *will* do something about it; others will not.

I have also met a number of people who say with deep sadness, "It's too late for me. I knew what was God's will— but I let the opportunities for service slip by." Of course it is never too late to do *something* for God and for others. So do not let the devil (or your own dillydallying) deter you. And do not wait till you "get around to doing something" about what you know is God's will.

*Produced by Paul Goodman, Missionary Enterprises, La Habra, California.

Some "going to" people are seminar haunters; they keep taking in and taking in. At a writers' conference, a conferee was called up to receive an award for having never missed that particular conference in its fifteen-year history. Congratulating her, I said naively, "What a lot of writing you must have done. What are you working on right now?"

"Oh," she replied, "I haven't done any writing yet—but *I'm going to* one of these days."

As a means of motivating people who have genuine talent and are procrastinating about using it, I have found something that works. I remind them that God will hold us all accountable for our stewardship of the gifts He has entrusted to us. To make it graphic, I ask them to imagine this scene: We are standing before the Lord, and He asks us, "What is that in your hand?" The writers answer, "A pencil, Lord." When He further probes, "What did you do with it?" will you have to hang your head and say, "I chewed the end of the pencil while I was waiting for the right time to get around to writing"? More than one person has later told me that this was what God used to break them of the self-defeating procrastination that had shackled them. The first step toward victory is recognizing the enemy.

Regret over what we have not done is almost universal. I see it again and again in the eyes of people who listen as I read this soul-searching poem:

HIS PLAN FOR ME

When I stand at the judgment seat of Christ,
  And He shows me His plan for me,
The plan of my life as it might have been
  Had He had His way, and I see

81

How I blocked Him here, and I checked Him there,
   And I would not yield my will . . .
Will there be grief in my Savior's eyes,
   Grief, though He loves me still?

He would have me rich, and I stand there poor,
   Stripped of all but His grace
While memory runs like a haunted thing
   Down the paths I cannot retrace. . . .

If that were the whole of the poem, I would keep it to my-self. It would be altogether too devastating and hopeless. And I would never want to be guilty of peddling discouraging, end-of-the-road philosophy. Nor need I here, for there are four more lines in this poem:

Lord, of the years that are left to me,
   I give *them* to Thy hand;
Take me and break me, mold me
   To the pattern Thou hast planned.

AUTHOR UNKNOWN

Here is a healthy reaction to the realization that, yes, we have wasted time, have passed up opportunities. But there is still today, and, it is hoped, tomorrow. We can still know the plus of finding what God has for us to do and doing it well.

8

WHY DOESN'T GOD *DO* SOMETHING?:

The Plus of Acceptance

Why is it, I have often asked myself, *that believers tend to be so slow to grasp certain principles of Christian living?* For instance, we are so prone to question God's will when things go contrary to what we would have chosen.

Some years ago, when I was having my own struggles along that line, the Lord gave me answers that satisfied my, "Why, God?" So, to share the help I had been given, I wrote a booklet titled *Acceptance Spells Peace.* Almost as soon as it was distributed, I began to receive letters in response. How well I remember the first. It came from heartbroken parents whose son had been given a verdict of six months to live. A college student not yet twenty years old, he was a victim of bone cancer. The mother wrote, "God has given our son wonderful peace, and though we feel crushed at the thought that he may not even live to finish out his school year, we too have a strange peace in our hearts."

What so impressed me, however, was this: "Our friends and relatives can't understand why we're not raging at God for this tragic waste of our son's life." The mother continued, "And we had no answers for them till we received this little booklet."

That was in 1972, and to this day there is a continuing demand for the booklet, indicating that obviously a great number of Christians are tangling with the same problem that absorbed me for many months.

The booklet applied the five Ws and the H of journalism to the problem of suffering: who, what, why, when, where, and how.

*W*ho am I that I should have to undergo such traumatic experiences?

*W*hat have I done that God let this happen to me?

*W*hy—why—and more why's?

*W*hen is God going to solve my problems?

*W*here can I find real help?

*H*ow can I cope in the meantime?

Far from rebuking me for my faithless questioning, the God who is slow to anger and of great compassion was patient and loving with me. Gradually I came to the comforting truth that *God knows what He is doing in our lives,* even when we do not. As Dr. Ralph Byron frequently tells his Sunday school class, "God uses tribulation to polish us." Paul knew this to be true when he wrote out of deep experience, "Our light affliction, which is but for a moment, worketh for us a far more exceeding and eternal weight of glory" (2 Corinthians 4:17).

In essence, Paul was saying, "It's not pleasant, but it has future rewards. Thanks, God."

Does this, perhaps, strike you as something of a Pollyanna attitude? Are you thinking, *Next thing you know she'll be quoting, "All things work together for good"?*

How can trouble or trial turn out for the best?

That is a normal, human question. And some people are really disturbed by it. They wonder if others are being strictly honest when they say, "Thank you, God, for sending me this trial." To them that seems a bit counterfeit, or at best hyperpious.

Because it is a fact of life that no one completely escapes trials and problems, it is certainly worth thinking over how a Christian should act—and react—in the midst of them.

What are the options?

A trial comes, some problem confronts us—and two courses are open to each one of us. We can resist. Or we can accept what comes our way.

A form of resistance, though not always recognized as such, is allowing ourselves to sink into a slough of despond. There, self-pity, first cousin to despondency, soon sucks us still further down, until we are wallowing in it. Our song is, "Poor me. No one ever had to bear such a trial as I'm going through. God must have forgotten me or forsaken me."

By reacting to trouble in that fashion, we are virtually criticizing God, verbally doubting His love, and downgrading His ability to care for us even if He does still love us. In a sense we are tossing God's promises in His face.

All that does is compound the problem. For now, in addition to having to handle it on our own, we are deliberately fracturing our relationship with the Lord. Surely doubt and disbelief grieve the Holy Spirit of God. In fact, *we can only grieve one who loves us*, so how much power is ours to grieve the very heart of God with our doubting of His love. We might ask ourselves, *What has God ever done that we, His people, don't trust Him?*

The alternative course?

Acceptance. We can take the circumstance and in faith say, "Thanks, God. I know it will work out for good." At the time it may take all the faith we can muster to enable us to see the silver lining in the clouds. It is true that we do not know at times why God sends trials our way. But faith's alternative to, "Why?" is "Thank You, God"—even when, smarting under the blow of circumstances, we may feel more like defiantly striking back than saying, "Thank You."

Built into an attitude of acceptance is our acknowledgment that God is working out His will in our lives.

> He knows, He loves, He cares,
> Nothing this truth can dim,
> He gives the very best to those
> Who leave the choice with Him.
>
> AUTHOR UNKNOWN

So, in accepting what God sends our way we are telling Him, "I know You are sovereign. You created me. Through faith in Your Son I became a member of Your family—and You are love. Even though I do not understand this particular thing You're doing in my life, I know You, Lord. I know You have my interests at heart, and that You are doing this for my ultimate good."

Moreover, has it ever occurred to you that God does not have to explain His actions to us any more than the potter has to explain to the clay he is molding. God does not have to answer our often petulant, "Why?" Many times He does sooner or later reveal why, but faith does not sit back, withholding acceptance until we have the explanation.

With the commitment of our way to God comes a draining of any resentment or rebellion against our circumstances. And that magic of acceptance is more than a spiritual concept or theory. As many in the field of psychiatry and psychology have long known, and some are just beginning to recognize, acceptance engenders peace.

Amy Carmichael, in one of her unforgettable poems, expresses that so eloquently.

IN ACCEPTANCE LIETH PEACE

He said, "I will forget the dying faces;
The empty places,
They shall be filled again.
O Voices moaning deep within me, cease."
But vain the word; vain, vain:
Not in forgetting lieth peace.

He said, "I will crowd action upon action,
The strife of faction
Shall stir me and sustain;
O tears that drown the fire of manhood cease."
But vain the word; vain, vain:
Not in endeavour lieth peace.

He said, "I will withdraw me and be quiet,
Why meddle in life's riot?
Shut be my door to pain.
Desire, thou dost befool me,
Thou shalt cease."
But vain the word; vain, vain:
Not in aloofness lieth peace.

87

He said, "I will submit; I am defeated.
God hath depleted
My life of its rich gain.
O futile murmurings, why will ye not cease?"
But vain the word; vain, vain:
Not in submission lieth peace.

He said, "I will accept the breaking sorrow
Which God tomorrow
Will to His son explain."
Then did the turmoil deep within him cease.
Not vain the word, not vain:
For in acceptance lieth peace.

At times, it takes less fortitude and endurance to accept death than to accept what life brings. I am reminded of a particularly fine-looking young man named Charles. As I sat with him on a Christian campus, and we went over the outline for his doctoral dissertation, he told me his story. He had been a noted athlete in his native Tanzania. One evening following a special performance, he and other national champions were feted at a victory celebration. Enroute home, their vehicle was demolished as a truck plowed into them. Of the thirteen top athletes, Charles alone escaped death to lie in a hospital, shattered in body and bitter in spirit for nearly a year.

"Why didn't God let *me* die?" was his continual, resentful cry.

But a Christian nurse patiently ministered to him and, although often discouraged, faithfully assured Charles that God did love Him, God did care. And one day that tall, handsome African opened his long-closed heart and let Jesus wash away the bitterness. He was born again. But never again would he be the champion gymnast, winning national acclaim. It was one thing to accept Christ as his Savior; it was another thing to accept the fact of a lifelong limp. Nevertheless, that day came in Charles's life. When I met him, there was on his face a radiance and a quiet peace I will not soon forget. One obvious sign of his acceptance of God's will is that he can enjoy his fellow students' athletic prowess and cheer them on, even though he himself has to walk with a cane. His witness, meanwhile, is a continuing inspiration to faculty and students alike.

They Can't Take It from You

God's peace. Peace the world could not give at the time Jesus spoke of it. And with all our genius, all our inventions, research, and science, the world has still not come up with that brand of peace or anything approximating it.

One day my mind was toying with this thought: what if the world's experts should somehow produce a formula for the peace of God (everyone is searching for peace, and such a discovery would certainly make the world's headlines). In light of the world's money and power struggles, we might foresee something like this happening:

A committee would be formed to regulate the formula; a bill would be passed in the legislature; the peace formula would be scrutinized in a test tube; next it would be formulated into a prescription, packaged, and marketed. The cost of advertising would price it out of reach of many who need it; it would be available only when the stores were open; it might be out of stock at times. Ultimately someone would come up with a synthetic version. And who is to say that the "peace of God formula" would not be eventually outlawed as "not in the public interest"?

Whimsical thinking? Yes. But it made me appreciate all the more the peace of God that the world cannot give, nor can it take it away. The peace of God is past understanding, as we read in Philippians 4:7. Likewise past understanding is the Christian whose heart and mind is kept by God's peace even in the midst of adverse circumstances.

I admit that it is still a great *mystery* to me that the peace of God can and does keep our hearts and minds in Christ Jesus. But it is not a *problem,* for God's Word tells me it is so. I do not have to know how God does this. That reminds me of something my brother told me regarding his seminary days. A godly professor of theology would say to his students when they were overly concerned about some "unknown": "Gentlemen, kindly allow God to know some things you don't know."

One of the greatest discoveries I have made as a believer is that the Christian can know real peace—genuine soul-and-mind-calming peace, *even while the problem still exists.* The open secret: *acceptance.*

Missionary Amy Carmichael wrote well and truly. Acceptance does beget peace; acceptance has both emotional and physical ramifications, in addition to the better-recognized spiritual benefits. For it takes emotional energy to fight an inward battle. The same measure of acceptance applied to the situation would leave us in a much better state to be able to deal with it.

WHY DOES ACCEPTANCE BRING SUCH POSITIVE RESULTS?

We may not know or understand all the dynamics at work.

But when we know God and trust Him, we realize that He knows what is best for us.

It is no idle whim that causes God to bid us give thanks in everything. And note the little word "in". Is God saying, "While the trial is still upon you, be thankful" (not only at some later time when we may be able to look back upon it as for our good, but also during the testing time)?

So, *in* everything it is good to give thanks to God.

I used to comfort myself that the Bible does not say, *"For everything, we should give thanks."* But how could I have bypassed Ephesians 5:20: *"Giving thanks always for all things"?*

I do not know which is harder, giving thanks in everything or for everything. But I do know that God's Word exhorts us to do both. And many times obedience is its own reward.

Giving thanks, and practicing acceptance cannot be separated. Saying, "Thanks, God. I needed that," has in it seeds of faith and hope as well as gratitude: faith that God is working out His plan in our lives and hope for a good outcome because our Father can be trusted to do what is best for us.

That is where Romans 8:28 with its "all things work together for good" comes in. The individual components of a situation in which we find ourselves may not be good, but as God works them together they produce His good design. Any homemaker can readily understand that concept (as we have developed it in chapter 4). The same principle holds true in many other areas. A single ingredient of a doctor's prescription might prove lethal; but let the prescribed components be mixed together and allowed to "work together," and the result is for the patient's good.

When we see that, we can be thankful for what God is doing with us, in us, and through us. When we accept what He sends, when we cast all the responsibility·for what happens to us upon God, we are conserving rather than draining our own resources. More than that, we find that in thus casting our burdens on the Lord, we actually recharge our spiritual and emotional batteries. And that is reflected in our physical well-being also.

Who would question the value of a calm attitude in time of crisis? Christians should mirror that calm more than anyone else. Why is it, then, that many of us fail to appropriate the great potential that is ours?

The Question of the Ages

The question arises, Must we expect trials as Christians? Does God delight in showering trouble on us?

No, of course He does not. Nevertheless, the Scriptures honestly and realistically prepare us to expect trouble: "In the world ye shall have tribulation" (John 16:33). The implication seems to be that tribulation goes hand in hand with our being in the world, that human beings simply by being alive can expect some trials. That applies to both Christian and unbeliever, as evidenced by Job's statement, "Man is born unto trouble, as the sparks fly upward" (Job 5:7). I like what C. S. Lewis said in *Surprised by Joy* (New York: Harcourt, Brace & World, 1955): "Straight tribulation is easier to bear than tribulation which advertises itself as pleasure."

Sometimes a new convert gets the impression, *Now that I have accepted Christ as my Savior, I won't have any more problems.* Older Christians do the "babes" an injustice when (knowingly or not) they create such an impression. They are merely adding to the number who have asked throughout history, "Why should the righteous suffer?"

The apostle Paul was a realist. He had not forgotten what he was told at the onset of his Christian life when he was shown what "great things he must suffer" for the name of Jesus (Acts 9:16). Far from resisting the idea of trials in the new life on which he had embarked, Paul accepted suffering as a badge of his identification with his Lord. He would say to us what he said to the Christians in Philippi: "To you has been given the privilege not only of trusting Him but also of suffering for him" (Philippians 1:29, TLB).

Suffering, a *privilege!*

Some believers are called upon to suffer more than others. There is a school of suffering where, it seems, God educates those whom He calls to bear particular trials. Enrolled in that school, we can be sure we have the master Teacher.

God is also the master Designer. He created us. It follows, then, that He knows best how to mold us. God is not toying with ceramics; He is shaping us for eternity with Him. Part of shaping involves painful experiences. One poet has likened God's patterning process to the weaver and the cloth he is looming:

> Not till the loom is silent
> And the shuttle has ceased to fly;
> And God has unrolled the canvas
> And explained the reason why
> The dark threads are as needful
> In the weaver's skillful hands,

93

As the threads of gold and silver
In the pattern *He* has planned.

AUTHOR UNKNOWN

We will never understand it, but there is a divine alchemy that produces sweetness out of sorrow, peace out of pain, and beauty for ashes. Yet who will dispute that that is so? The serenity on the face of the chronic sufferer, the peace-filled expression when pain furrows the brow would be more understandable to the bystander. Those eloquently voice another truth Paul came to see: "My grace is sufficient for thee" (2 Corinthians 12:9).

Unquestionably the most difficult thing to accept—to thank God for—is death. We know that it is appointed unto man once to die. We know that to die is gain, that absence from the body means being present with the Lord. As Christians we would strongly defend our position on that truth. But we have emotions to deal with. Our emotions affirm for us that the last enemy is death, and we shrink from that enemy.

The medical profession has long known that normally there are three reactions on the part of someone who realizes (or is told) that his death is imminent. The first is unbelief. "Everybody dies. I know that. But not me—not now!" The second reaction is that the patient looks around for someone to blame. The physician comes in for more than his share of that blame. "There must be something you've done or failed to do for me, doctor." Third is acceptance. After a while, when the idea of dying has become somewhat less of a shock, some people are able to draw from an inner reserve the ability to accept the fact that their remaining days on earth will be few. And with that acceptance—that cease-fire with regard to the inevitable—comes a measure of peace.

Clearly, then, it should follow that when the patient is a true believer in Christ, as he accepts his impending departure from this life, his peace will be the peace that Jesus gives. He will be enveloped in it, knowing that neither life nor death can separate him from the love of God that is in Christ Jesus (see Romans 8:38-39).

Not all trials, however, come in the form of physical suffering. Some are emotional, some may even be spiritual, and for some people trials are a combination of all three. But, ultimately, whatever the problem, if there is to be healing there first must be acceptance.

Then, because God is the Author of order and purpose, the one who has been enabled to triumph over suffering begins to see what God had in mind in permitting the trial. A new spiritual awareness emerges and with it a new compassion for others.

Many Christians can live a lifetime without coming to understand how powerful is God's Word, how unfailing His promises. I might have been one of them, for I had really felt God was doing me a favor—was being good to me— in not letting life buffet me. I know better now. For, in His love and wisdom God did send circumstances that threatened to knock the spiritual "props" from under me. Rebellion, resentment against God, self-pity, depression—I have been through them all. Meanwhile the covenant-keeping God did not forsake me. It took time for me to see anything for which to be thankful. As for acceptance, it was a gradual process, but with the ability to accept what God had permitted there came new joy, new understanding of the love

95

of God, a new relationship with Him, and new ability to understand other people and to be compassionate toward them. *The Living Bible* beautifully paraphrases 2 Corinthians 1:3-4:

> What a wonderful God we have—he is the Father of our Lord Jesus Christ, the source of every mercy, and the one who so wonderfully comforts and strengthens us in our hardships and trials. And why does he do this? So that when others are troubled, needing our sympathy and encouragement, we can pass on to them this same help and comfort God has given us.

The truth of those words is personalized for us. We see God's sweet uses of adversity when in acceptance we have found His peace.

Because God has made us what we are, *reasoning* human beings, we shall always have a "Why" until that day when we shall "know as we are known." Until then, however, we can trust in what Paul describes as the "good, and acceptable" will of God for our lives (Romans 12:2).

9

SERENE AND SATISFIED:

The Plus of a Contented Spirit

The church soloist was singing a hymn that was new to me. Each stanza ended with, "I have a contented heart." Listening, I said to myself, *She knows what she is singing about.* For I have long been acquainted with that woman. She has undergone severe, persistent physical suffering, yet there is about her a pervasive air of contentment. And even when the suffering is reflected in her eyes, she has a smile.

How many such people do you know?

According to Henry Ward Beecher, "We see in a lifetime only a dozen or so faces marked with the peace of a contented spirit."

He may have been right.

What is contentment, and what difference does it make whether we have it or not?

Perhaps the purest definition is "satisfaction." The contented person is not striving for something external to provide satisfaction. He has it on the inside. There is a peace, a calm spirit about that person, which makes all the difference in the world to the individual and to those around him.

Discontented people know no such inner peace. They do not experience feelings of inner satisfaction. They are

97

restless, tending often to think that other people's lot in life is easier than their own. There is a "grass is greener on the other side" philosophy. And they frequently blame their circumstances for their discontent. You have met them and so have I. "Joe" complains, "It's all right for *you* to talk about being content, but if you had my problems—" Then there is "Anne." She grumbles, "If only I could have what so-and-so has, how easy it would be for me to live a contented life."

Both Joe and Anne are Christians, earnest workers in their church. Sadly, they are representative of a host of other believers (maybe you and me) who at times gripe at what God sends our way. At such times we are "under the circumstances." Actually, however, circumstances have very little to do with having a contented spirit.

WE'RE NOT BORN CONTENTED

You might question, Are some people born with that admirable spirit of contentment, and others not?

The answer is no, as Paul makes amply clear in Philippians 4:11: "I have learned, in whatsoever state I am, therewith to be content."

"Whatsoever state" can have to do with our geographical state—wherever the Lord leads us; it can be applied to our physical state—whatever the condition of our health; and it can pertain to our economic condition—whatever the state of our finances.

Apparently Christians do not automatically have such a conviction and such a stable attitude toward contentment. We were not born with it; it does not necessarily come even with conversion. "I have learned," Paul admits. Surely he had more than his share of opportunities to test his level of contentment under all circumstances.

The attaining of a contented spirit is, then, a growing, learning experience.

Some people learn life's lessons quicker than others. They display earlier the Christian maturity that is marked by a contented spirit. For instance, I confess that at my age I am still working on *patience*. I tap my foot just waiting for the traffic light to change. But, since impatience and contentment are quite incompatible, I am not going to quit trying, with God's help, to conquer my impatience.

Why would one person learn more readily than another in similar circumstances?

As in all phases of learning, there has to be (1) a willingness to learn, and (2) access to resources for learning.

If we find that we are slow learners—slow to mature toward contentment—that is a problem we can take to the Lord. We can pray, "Lord, please help me to *want* to learn your ways." As for resources, we have the unlimited power of the Holy Spirit, one of whose missions is to reveal truth to us and teach us (John 16:13-14). We also have the Word of God, which spells out for us what the Lord would have us to be. "He will teach us of his ways" (Micah 4:2).

I have long been impressed that God is more concerned with what we are—our *be*ing, than He is with what we do— our *do*ing. We have in the Bible a group of verses we call the Beatitudes (for emphasis, I sometimes split the word: Be-attitudes); but can you give me chapter and verse for the *Do*attitudes? Granted, we do what we do because of what we are; nevertheless, it would appear that God is vastly concerned with our attitudes.

I think of an older woman I knew in Canada. She had the most serene face I have ever seen; she oozed contentment. As a new Christian I met her in the warm fellowship of a Saturday evening group, and I can still hear her singing, "I have Christ; what want I more?"* The words she sang were totally believable because she lived her life by them. What an ornament of grace such a person is!

Sometimes we sing about the deep, settled peace in our souls. But what if we never experienced irksome, difficult times? If we never know the frustration of undesirable circumstances, how should we ever know for sure whether or not we have the peace we have sung about?

I am inclined to think that at times we need to get outside our usual situations in order to find out where our anchor is really fixed and if it will indeed weather the storms of life. It may be good to deliberately venture into something new, where the normal props that keep us steady may not be present. Not that I would advocate some foolish undertaking that would fall into the category of "presumptuous sins"; rather I have in mind taking some risks for God. How else can we prove for ourselves that what was true in Paul's day can be equally true for the Christian in our own times? What validity would there be in my saying, "I am content in whatever state I find myself," if my state remains static? I could be fooling myself as to the source, the quality, and the dependability of my "contented spirit."

A biblical formula for the serene and satisfied life, something I call a divine equation, is:

$$\text{Godliness} + \text{Contentment} = \text{Great Gain}$$
(see 1 Timothy 6:6).

*Author unknown.

100

Godly. To how many people do you attribute that word? I reserve that adjective for a very few people I have known. My feeling for those people is mixed with special admiration and, yes, a little awe. Henry Ward Beecher may have been quite accurate in his supposition that we meet not more than a dozen such Christians in a lifetime. Yet, think what that combination of godliness and contentment produces—"great gain." Something that many people strive for a lifetime to attain.

(It needs to be said that there is a place for a certain degree of *dis*content, such as when we are in danger of feeling that "spiritually I have arrived." Here is where giving heed to Paul's words, "Not as though I had already attained. . . . I press toward the mark" [Philippians 3:12-15] can help to keep us in balance.)

Nevertheless, a worthy goal for the maturing believer is to possess the great gain that is godliness and contentment.

THE PLUS OF A CONTENTED SPIRIT

Did God intend that great gain to be reserved for the few—that dozen you and I might meet in our lifetimes? I think not. Surely God does not have His predetermined spiritual millionaires whose countenances mirror their gain. So why cannot you and I share in the great gain? What hinders us from being such people? First Timothy 6:6-12 provides clues for us.

Writing to his "son Timothy," *in the context of contentment* Paul exhorts the young man to flee from the world's standards of gain, from the snare and corrupting influence of the *love* of money (not money itself), and to follow hard after righteousness, godliness, faith, love, patience, meekness

101

(sound like "the fruit of the Spirit"?). That makes me think of Dr. Raymond Ortlund's oft repeated earnest plea, *"Go hard after God!"*

So there is no secret to that divine equation—and it is for us today, a plus of obeying God's Word and living in the Spirit.

THE MINUS OF DISCONTENT

What about the times when we are not content, when we fuss and fume, grumble and gripe, whine and whimper? That, too, shows on our countenances. It is displayed in frown lines, in unsmiling visages that turn people from us. It is to be regretted that our discontent may also turn them from Christ, because they view us as models of the Christian life. Whether we realize it or not, we are constantly projecting an image, either positive or negative. And, have you thought that even though you may be going through a particularly trying experience (one common to Christian and non-Christian), your non-Christian neighbors expect that you will be able to handle it better than they can?

One day as I pondered that anomaly, the Lord gave me this flash of insight: since those outside Christ have such high standards for and expectations of the professing believer in Christ (and, reasonably or unreasonably, they do!) it must be that they have a desperate need for what they think "being a believer in Christ" provides. I mean that in the areas of peace of mind and the ability to cope with the stresses of life.

When we have witnessed to friends or neighbors, what a letdown it must be for them to see us as "failing to deliver" by collapsing in the way they would likely do themselves in the same situation.

In the days before the clothes dryer, one breezy spring morning I had just loaded my backyard lines when down one of them sagged. My Tide-clean wash was dragged in the mud from a recent rain. I forgot all about Romans 8:28. At that moment I was *furious,* and in her yard my unsaved neighbor heard my tirade against the wind, the manufacturers of clotheslines, and so on.

It took time for me to undo the impression I had created in her mind that day I allowed myself to get "under the circumstances." But I learned a lesson.

FOES OF A CONTENTED SPIRIT

I would not presume to suggest I have all the answers. I would just like to share from experience and observation some of the enemies that rob us of the contentment that can be ours.

1. *Fighting the inevitable* uses up our energy in battling something over which we have no control. For instance, not long ago I heard two men—I'll call them Tom and Jack—discussing that very thing. Both are bright, intelligent Christians. Jack had a grim look as he spilled out his frustrations. Seemingly the problem had to do with an irresponsible employee, who was either unaware of or did not care how his behavior was affecting his boss and other employees.

Tom's response to Jack's complaint was almost casual. "I have the same problem lots of times," he said, "but I don't fight what I can't change. I find it pays to keep calm and go about my own business."

As the conversation progressed, Jack, still tense, fumed, "Well, *I* haven't come to the place where I don't fight it." His face was the picture of discontent, whereas Tom's mirrored his inner serenity.

What are the down-to-earth advantages of *not* fighting the inevitable? Invited as the speaker for a women's retreat on an army post, I gained some new insights. I had not been involved with the military, so these women had much to teach me. In a talking time around the camp fireplace, the topic *moving* came up. All the women participated, for most of them had experienced multiple uprootings of their families through army orders. Listening, I was impressed with how, as *Christian* wives, some viewed these orders and handled the situations, which must always have meant some trauma for family members. One officer's wife, who could have been speaking for the rest, expressed her feelings:

"Although my husband's orders are issued by the Department of the Army," she explained, "I feel that for us as a Christian family they are also *God's* orders for us. The move is in His will, is part of His overall plan for our lives. So we don't fight it, even though sometimes we would *love* to stay put."

I could not help thinking what a positive effect that attitude must have on the wife herself, on her officer husband, and upon their children. Boys and girls learn attitudes from their parents; what if all they ever heard from Mom was, "Why do I have to be an *army* wife? If your Dad was only in some other work, we could settle down instead of always having to be at the beck and call of the army."

Such thinking would almost certainly rub off on the children (that applies whatever the father's occupation). **One** of the logical reasons for accepting mandatory changes is, in the words of another woman at the retreat, "I knew he was in the army when I married him." Logic and reason, however, are rarely a part of the malcontented person's thinking.

As I spent a weekend with those service wives, I sensed that a number of them at least had learned not only to submit to God's will, but also to make the most and the best of what comes their way in life. That is true contentment—and it will be reflected in their lives wherever they go "on army orders." With Paul they can say *literally,* "I have learned, in whatever state (or foreign country) I find myself, therewith to be content."

2. Sometimes we can find a foe of a contented spirit just by looking in the mirror. We can be our own worst enemy. That is true when we permit *doubts* to lodge in our minds, when we let ourselves grumble and dwell on lesser things than we need to, rather than on God's daily goodness.

Have you ever thought that discontent has an associated vocabulary, a set of words all beginning with *d,* words that paint dreary, dismal images in our minds? There is disillusionment, despair, disappointment, despondency, depression, and, as we have already mentioned, doubt. Those are all pessimistic words. The more we let ourselves dwell on them, the more they will rob us of the plus of contentment.

We have to contend with such mental images in their early stages. It is good to tell ourselves that temporary despondency does not mean we have to slump further down. Rather, we need to conquer it before it conquers us.

3. Another common foe of contentment is *self-pity,* that "poor me" attitude that blinds us to the present blessings around us. To be sure, all of us at times are prey to such

feelings. It is the chronic preoccupation with them that is so debilitating and emotionally destructive.

But what to do about it?

When I feel a low mood coming on, I realize I had better recognize it for what it is and do something to combat it— do *anything* rather than just dwelling on my feelings. A brisk walk is a fine antidote, but that is not always possible. However, there are always things around the house that I have been putting off. I tackle one of them and find, as I assure you that you will, that just accomplishing some little task generates a feeling of well-being. On one such day I came across a Bible verse I had not really noticed before. In Psalm 3:3, David encourages us, "Thou, O LORD, art . . . the lifter up of mine head."

Ultimately, God is the only One who can keep us from becoming enmeshed in negative feelings. But He also graciously gives us the ability to help "keep ourselves on an even keel."

4. Still another foe is *perpetually dwelling on the past.* "In my last job I was [this or that]." "The last place we lived in was a thousand times better than this." "The people at our last church were more friendly." Everything "before" was "more." The person might just as well be wearing a lapel pin reading, "I'm not contented; I don't like it here."

Discontent is a subtle irritant and must be confronted. The time to grapple with it is when we catch ourselves *to an excessive degree* comparing the present unfavorably with past circumstances. We need to be honest with ourselves. Naturally, we all have times of nostalgia, times when previous days are colored in our thoughts so as to appear to have been always good. That, however, is more a matter of memory playing tricks on us than our being discontented with what is now.

It is wise to ask when we feel discontent, what is *causing* such feelings. Then let us be specific in answering ourselves.

Sometimes when I am a victim of discontent, I stop what I am doing, grab pencil and paper, and write down my thoughts at the time, trying to be as objective as possible. I also jot down the date. When I have later come across those "gripe notes," I have been amazed at the feelings recorded. To be sure, things may have changed in the interim. But more often I have realized that I had grown up a little. I am able to see that a particularly discontented period may have been just a mood, that maybe even the weather had contributed to how I was feeling. Or (a big factor for everyone in our family) the mail that day had not been interesting or exciting). Both circumstances could have changed by the next day. Yet, according to my own say-so, I had settled for the minus of discontent.

A question I now ask myself when I sense a lack of serenity is, *Do I honestly want to do something myself to change whatever it is that's bothering me? Or am I expecting everyone else to rally and change things to suit me?*

Then, too, it is good to acknowledge our discontent to the Lord. Why? Because, in a sense, with every breath of dissatisfaction we are murmuring ultimately against God Himself. In effect, we are saying, "God, You haven't done a very good job of making my day." That is the time to confess our sin and accept God's forgiveness, then shake off the negative feelings and say *aloud*, "This *is* the day that the Lord has made. I will be glad and rejoice in it."

Note the "I will." Everything we accomplish is accomplished because we first will to do it. So let us resolve, I *will not* complain, I *will not* feel sorry for myself, I *will not* think of the past as always being better than today. (Add any other resolutions that will counteract your own tendency toward discontentment.) *I will* be content with such things as I have. As the Reverend Kenneth Haystead, a radio pastor, has said: "One secret of contentment is knowing how to enjoy what you have today."

In summary we can ask ourselves, *Have I committed today to the Lord? Did I really mean it? Was I saying from my heart, "Lord, please take charge of my life today"?*

If we are indeed earnest about that—just one day at a time—it follows that whatever the day brings, we will be content with it. Otherwise would there not be something false in the "commitment" of our day to the Lord?

We can trust God to do His part. In return we can be content with such things as He sees fit to send our way.

Because God knows the human propensity for becoming discontented, we have the assurance, "Thou wilt keep him in perfect peace, whose mind is stayed on thee: because he trusteth in thee" (Isaiah 26:3).

Perfect peace—serenity—and satisfaction. They *can* be yours and mine.

10

EXPRESSION OR REPRESSION:

The Plus of Balanced Emotions

Did this "open" generation invent emotions? Sometimes it would seem so, but that is not true.

The God who created us *physical* beings and breathed into man the breath of life that makes us *spiritual* beings, likewise endowed us with an *emotional* dimension.

Yet among Christians there are certainly two schools of thought concerning that area of our humanity. One group would advocate almost total repression of feelings, whereas the other would vote for uninhibited expression.

Somewhere between those two lies the balance.

Some time ago I heard a speaker at a Christian conference decry any and all display of emotion. "There's too much of that these days," she said, then added, "I'm sure I 'emote' as much as God ever intended we should. But I'm careful to keep my feelings to myself."

I wondered at the time, and I still do, what the woman meant to imply by "as much as God intended," and what were the emotions in the rest of us with which she was displeased.

How can we read God's intentions for other people in the realm of human emotions?

Why, in certain Christian circles, is any display of emotion frowned upon?

Let us think of the first two aspects of the fruit of the Spirit, love and joy (Galatians 5:22). What are those if they are not emotions? And how would we go about expressing that we are loving, or that our hearts are overflowing with the joy of the Lord, while repressing all display of emotion?

Take out those verses about love and joy and what a hole we would leave in the Scriptures. Believers cannot be *for* the fruit of the Spirit and *against* showing it in their lives. It is good to realize that God gave us our emotions. They are part of our being "fearfully and wonderfully made" as we read in Psalm 139:14.

WHY ARE SOME MORE EMOTIONAL THAN OTHERS?

Sometimes we hear said of a person, "He is so emotional." What is meant is that such people show their feelings. They may not *be* any more emotional than others.

Many factors determine human behavior. Not always do we take that into consideration when we view how other people act. The woman who was squelching her fellow Christians was making no allowance whatever for the fact that we are all different.

Heritage helps shape how we will express or repress our emotions. Of Scottish background, I grew up with people who are notably restrained. "Typical British restraint," the commentators dub the trait. Yet, Scottish people are really very sentimental; our poets and songwriters say it for us.

New Englanders are another conservative breed, not given as a group to a display of feelings. (There are always those who are exceptions and break out of the mold.)

110

Perhaps *climate* is a contributor to how people show their feelings, for it seems that the warmer areas produce more openly emotional men and women—the Latin countries in particular.

The *model* we were given in childhood is a strong determinant of our future behavior and attitudes. Undemonstrative parents are likely to have undemonstrative children.

Whatever our background, we can change. Here is where I part company with the psychologist who asserts that childhood patterns inexorably mold one's whole life. I side, rather, with those "experts" who agree that although we are products of our past, we are not prisoners of it. We can break out.

Let me say here that I in no way advocate that we all suddenly become highly emotional. Emotion simply for emotion's sake can be properly suspect as superficial or even false.

EMOTIONS TO PUT OFF

Another aspect to consider is the paradoxical twist in some Christians' ideas about emotions. Although they would guard against any show of love or joy, they seem to have no such prohibitions against negative emotions—unrestrained anger, for instance.

Are we, then, to rationalize that negative emotions and the display of them are God intended? I read in Ephesians 4 that we should put off or put away such things. Nowhere in Scripture do I read to put off love and kindred emotions.

Why the injunction to put away anger? Obviously because of the potential for sinning when we are angry. In the heat of anger we say things that we do not really mean but

111

that we can never retract. That, in turn, gives rise to feelings of guilt, which keep us from being at our best.

Frequently we become vengeful ("I'll get even with you"), forgetting Romans 12:19, "Vengeance is mine; I will repay, saith the Lord." Not that God is vengeful, but He is the only One who can rightly judge a situation. It is because of His regard for us that He does not want us to assume what is rightfully His prerogative. He knows what an angry spirit does to us, and He would spare us its consequences.

The Bible is ever practical, however. And God knows we *will* become angry at times. To help us cope, He does not merely say, "Don't be angry." Rather, we read, "Be ye angry, *and sin not*" (Ephesians 4:26, italics added). So in the sight of God, it is not anger but what we do with it—what we let it do to our spirit—that constitutes sinning. I was a Christian for quite a few years before that teaching became clear to me.

Anger can work for us. Yes, it can. Far from causing us to feel like failures, to feel guilty and spiritually defeated, we can win over that emotion and emerge spiritually stronger, better equipped to meet Satan's next bout with us.

How does anger work for us? you may be asking.

It was a great forward step in my own spiritual growth when I began to understand that *as far as my emotions are concerned, I am in a position of choice.* I can say to myself, *Something has made you angry. Now what are you going to do about it?*

When the anger involves a personal encounter, I can will myself to keep quiet while I count to ten or however high I need to count in order to gain control of my anger. Then, shooting up a silent prayer for a calm spirit, I may say, "What

112

you've just done [or said] makes me very angry." (Note: Not *"You* make me angry." There is a difference.) Many times that reasonable approach creates the emotional climate for open discussion. The other person may respond, "Oh, I didn't realize—I didn't mean to make you angry," and what could otherwise have created a rift can be cleared up.

Not always is the person who sparked the anger immediately present. Sometimes a letter, telephone call, or some other circumstances arouses our ire. I recall a situation in which I was involuntarily caught up, and to this day I can remember how angry I was at the time. Right then there was no way I could confront the one who had triggered the anger; nor was there a reasonable way I could deal with the situation. So what did I do? While the adrenalin was flowing and energizing me, I dashed upstairs and attacked the bathroom. I gave it the most thorough scrubbing it had had in months. In scouring the bathroom so vigorously, I scoured the anger out of my system. No one was hurt. I had not added fuel to an already volatile situation. Rather, the anger had worked for me. I had something to show for it. Later, when it was opportune, the cause of that anger was dealt with appropriately. In such ways I am finding out that

> Each vict'ry will help you
> Some other to win.

H. R. PALMER

It *is* experientially possible to be angry and sin not.

Dealing with the anger prevents the buildup of smoldering hostility. Also—and this is a great plus—we have such a good feeling inside when, with the Lord's help, we manage to be angry and sin not. The reverse is all too true. Unre-

113

solved anger leads to many inner problems. Numerous psychologists and psychiatrists state categorically that *depression is anger turned on oneself.* Depression, with all of its debilitating ramifications!

How much better to appropriately express the anger than to repress it.

God bids us put away all malice and anger (Ephesians 4:31), and unlike even the best of Christian counselors, God also gives us the power to carry out His directives. "I can do all things through Christ which strengtheneth me" (Philippians 4:13).

Ephesians 4:26 goes on to exhort us, "Let not the sun go down upon your wrath." That is practical counsel for emotional health, for when we take unresolved angry feelings to bed with us, they will work on our subconscious all night long, and we shall wake up to start the new day in a still angry frame of mind. So one way to take good care of your emotional health is to treat an anger-causing situation as you would garbage. Get rid of it before it piles up on you.

Another form of anger is the *motivating* kind. To illustrate, you see someone ill-treating a child. Is it wrong to feel angry at such times? I once heard author Cynthia De Moss say, "Feelings give drive to human endeavor—make us *do* something; otherwise we are just 'all talk.' "

Our Lord displayed that type of anger when the very people who should have known better were making His Father's house a "den of thieves" (Matthew 21:13). Jesus was angry, and sinned not. He expressed, He did not repress, His feelings.

THE THERAPY OF GRIEF

Another emotion that tends to make some Christians

114

uneasy is grief (sometimes I wonder where we get our distorted concepts of acceptable-to-God attitudes). During most of my years as a believer, I have been given the idea that "a good Christian does not grieve" (at least outwardly). How wrong can we be? We gladly and unequivocably take our Lord Jesus Christ as an example in other areas of behavior. Why, then, do we so often bypass the fact that when death took one of His friends, Jesus openly wept—to the degree that bystanders observed to one another, "Behold how he loved him [Lazarus]" (John 11:35-36). Evidently Jesus had no inhibitions about displaying His feelings in public. By contrast, many Christians seemingly cannot permit themselves the release that tears bring, fearing they will be judged unspiritual.

I think of a pastor friend whose wife died suddenly. She had been active in the church and, with her husband, was dearly loved by the congregation. I remember so well the announcement of her funeral service, or memorial service, as that has come to be called. "Come, and wear your brightest colors as we celebrate her homegoing." Fine. The congregation was just following the teaching the pastor himself had given them for a score of years. Everyone did "the right thing"; the pastor bore up admirably, showed no grief openly, just "celebrated" with his people the death of his life partner.

Months later I chanced to be a guest in a home where this pastor was also visiting. I scarcely recognized the ghost of a man he had become. Deep sorrow over the snatching away of his loved wife, suppressed in the interests of Christian expectations of him, had worked its devastation. It had affected him both physically and emotionally (I was not in a position

115

to know if the damage was also spiritual).

Granted, that may seem an extreme example of the result of repressed emotions. But it is wholly true and only too representative of other such cases.

How much better when we weep as did Jesus at the grave of his friend Lazarus. True we "sorrow not, even as others which have no hope" (1 Thessalonians 4:13). But we do ourselves an emotional disservice when we place the period after "we sorrow not."

"Weeping may endure for a night," the Bible tells us (Psalm 30:5), "but joy cometh in the morning." When one is robbed of the release and relief of a "night of weeping," it may be many a morning before the promised joy takes over—if indeed it ever does.

It pays, then, to study, to heed, and to practice what God's Word teaches about our emotions.

BEING A PART OF THE HUMAN RACE

Vulnerability is an "ability" some people are hesitant to show.

What do I mean?

Many of us tend to be such "stiff upper lip" persons that we would never dream of letting another see or know about our problems. We thus come across as people who are never bothered by anything, or who do not need anyone to help us cope when something does disturb. Yet, it is when we *are* vulnerable, when we are hurting and let someone know, that we seem much more a part of the human race.

To whom do we go when we need a shoulder to cry on? Not to the one who never (apparently) has any such need himself. We view such a person as likely being unable to help because of lack of personal experience.

116

We go to the One who is "acquainted with grief," our Lord Himself, *because He knows all about our hurt*. It would seem, then, that in our need for human sympathy and comfort we would gravitate to one who has demonstrated some acquaintance with grief.

If we aspire to become a partner with God in a ministry of comfort and consolation, we will first have to show that we ourselves are vulnerable—a part of the human race.

LETTING AND FRETTING

One emotion capturing much attention these days is *anxiety*. It has become a catchall word, an umbrella sheltering a variety of emotional ills, and what might create anxiety in one Christian may have a greater or lesser effect on another. So we cannot be judgmental; only God knows the inner workings of our hearts. Some people appear to be congenital worrywarts. I used to be one of them. I could worry about anything—or nothing. That is known as "floating anxiety"; that is, it has no object to fasten on to. There is no known reason for the anxiety or worry.

Some anxieties are related to the times in which we live. These are days of unprecedented discoveries and inventions—some of them truly fearful. We live in fear of what we know and of what we do not know, unless we can manage to keep our ears tuned to God's "fear not." For nothing can catch God by surprise. He knows all about the things that are happening and their timing. He can and will keep us from undue anxieties.

A move in the right direction is to internalize the comfort offered in Philippians 4:6-7:

> Have no anxiety about anything, but in everything by prayer and supplication with thanksgiving let your requests

117

be made known to God. And the peace of God, which passes all understanding, will keep your hearts and your minds in Christ Jesus (RSV*).

Fretting is akin to anxiety (and it is not God's will for us). "Fret not . . . . fret not . . . . fret not." Three times we read that in the space of eight verses (Psalm 37:1, 7, 8).

The antidote to both anxiety and fretting is obviously the *peace of God*. It is almost impossible to appropriate God's peace and continue to fret and be anxious. The two attitudes are mutually exclusive.

"Let not" is another interesting prohibition in the context of our emotions. "Let not your heart be troubled." Twice our Lord encourages us with that exhortation in John 14, that emotion-packed chapter. And again clearly comes His promise of peace the world can neither give nor take away.

Christ's directive to us, "Let not," carries with it the intimation that "it's up to you"; you can let or not let your heart be at peace.

We find this again in Colossians 3:15, "Let the peace of God rule your hearts."

Some people have found that "letting" a reality in their lives. I know a woman who has a physical condition that makes her not very acceptable to the average person. She is aware of that and has a good understanding of the reasonableness of people's reactions. One day she said to me, when I was hurting for her because of the behavior of an insensitive person, "You know, Jeanette, nobody can hurt me *unless I let them.*" She had learned that salving truth that Jesus would teach all of us. Certainly, since we are assured that nothing can separate us from the love of Christ, we can

*Revised Standard Version.

118

lean hard on Him and *not let* what others do or say rob our day of its peace.

In summary, I would like to say this on the subject of balance in our display of emotions: God has made us with the capacity to *feel* and to *demonstrate* what we feel.

We will display our emotions largely on the basis of the kind of person God has made us and the background that has been ours, the "model" we have been given.

We need to *be aware* of the differences in people, which cause them to be either openly warm and loving or to be more restrained in expressing feelings. Such awareness can keep us from having critical or judgmental attitudes toward fellow Christians.

Personally, though conservative by nature, I would not want to revert to being a person who cannot show her emotions when it is appropriate to do so. A poem I wrote expresses something of what I am saying:

> It's easy to show
>   By the things that we do—
> The cooking, the cleaning
>   And ironing, too—
> That we love.
>   Why then to thc deeds
> Do we not add the three little words
>   I LOVE YOU?
>
>   So simple to voice
> Yet so strongly they speak
>   That they drown out our failings—
> Make others rejoice—
>   These three little words
> I love you.

119

I find myself pondering
How else had we heard
   Had not God, in His Word
Said, "I LOVE *YOU*."

11

UNDER HIS WINGS:

The Plus of Inner Security

It was the week following the showing of "The Holocaust" on national television. A panel of Jewish persons, some of whom had survived the Nazi horrors, were discussing the actual events in the light of the TV special.

I shall never forget what a younger woman (child of a couple who had survived) revealed of the deep, national insecurity of her people. Her face intense with thought, she said, "Somewhere in a corner of my mind I always have a bag packed."

Sad as that is to contemplate in that it indicates ultimate lack of security, the problem does not really touch most of our lives. "It's a Jewish matter. And that was *Europe*," we may say, thus disassociating ourselves from the problems of the Jews throughout the centuries.

Today however, there is mounting insecurity for millions of Americans. It is a great day for the locks and bolts and electronic safety devices industry. Meanwhile thousands of older people in our large cities are virtually prisoners of fear, rarely venturing out of their homes. Much of that fear is justified, to be sure, because violence is abroad both day and night. But besides that, there is a nameless, pervasive societal insecurity, a lack of trust in anything and anybody.

121

Fear is the enemy of inner security. And whether we are prepared to believe it or not, Christians are as prone to fear as unbelievers. Yet God's Word comes to us, "Fear not." I have heard reputable Bible teachers say that "fear not," in some form, appears 366 times in the Bible: one for every day—and an extra for Leap Year!)

PRESENT TENSE SECURITY

When I was a fairly new Christian, one of the most popular tracts was titled *Safety, Certainty and Security*. Was the title redundant? Are not safety, certainty, and security much the same thing? On the surface they appear to be so; they are assuredly intertwined. However, I am inclined to believe that security towers above the other two in significance.

"Why?" you may be asking.

To me, security leaves room for risking something. On the other hand, if I am certain of the outcome, that in itself is my security. If I am embarking on a safe venture, I do not need the reassurance of security.

But when I sense God through His Spirit directing me toward some "unknown," that is when I need to feel secure.

The disciples went out into the unknown.

The early church launched out with no certainties as to the future.

The apostle Paul ventured again and again into uncertainties.

What was *their* security? What was "safe" about their undertakings? How certain was any outcome of their efforts?

Nothing was safe, certain, and secure except one thing, and that was enough. Jesus had commissioned them; He had promised to be with them; He had promised never to leave them. That brings to mind something Bill Bright said recently. Speaking of the Great Commission, Mr. Bright remarked, "Jesus did not say, 'Go—and good luck!' He said, 'Go—and, lo, I am with you.' " I *am*—present tense.

With such assurance from the lips of their Lord, no wonder the disciples went forth undaunted—sheep among wolves—and in the power of the Holy Spirit turned the world upside down.

The Lord Jesus is still saying, "I am with you."

Have you thought how minutely God's Word spells out His care and concern for us? We are prone to think of God as intervening on our behalf in times of crisis. And He does. But we do not live out our days on the edge of a crisis. So how good it is to know that Jesus promised, "I am with you alway" (Matthew 28:20; I have heard "alway" translated "all the days"). That would mean the sunny days, the bleak days, the days of vigor and health, the days when sickness blights, the happy days, and the sad days. We can count on God *all the days*.

A newsman once asked Ethel Waters, "Why do you specially like to sing the 'Sparrow' song?"

"Why, bless your heart," she replied with a warm smile, "the sparrow am the *poverty* bird. And if God so cares for that little bird, then He is *never* gonna forget me and my people."

IT DOESN'T MEAN SAFETY

The Old Testament likewise gives us word portraits of people who did memorable exploits, yet had the promise of neither safety nor certainty.

Let us consider some of those heroes of the faith.

123

Abraham went out "not knowing whither he went." But he knew God, and he knew God was with him.

Moses set out on the most phenomenal of earth's pilgrimages, conducting through a hostile wilderness some two million Hebrews, many of them rebellious at times. To add to Moses' problems there were no service stops or supermarkets along the wilderness trail. What kept the emancipator going? He went at God's command, and one day when he needed special reassurance, the Lord said to him, "My presence shall go with thee" (Exodus 33:14).

Daniel "purposed in his heart" to counter the king's command—practically a suicidal venture in that day of absolute monarchs—to serve God rather than the king. Likewise Daniel's three friends braved the fiery furnace, confidently asserting that their God was able to deliver them. Even the thought "What if He doesn't?" had no effect on their faith. Their daring and steadfastness won them a place in history. "Dare to Be a Daniel" is the Christian's rallying cry for witnessing under fire.

Hebrews 11 memorializes many others who shunned safety, not counting their lives dear unto themselves.

What would have happened throughout the history of the Christian church had leaders and others done only the safe thing? Instead, they could venture without assurance of safety because they had God-given *inner security*.

A Modern-Day Fear

I have heard "experts" say that we enter this world with two fears: the fear of falling and the fear of loud noises.

Each era breeds its specialized causes of fear. One of

those for many people in our age is the fear of flying. I am surprised at times to learn that an acquaintance whom I know to be a poised, confident, and competent person nevertheless dreads traveling by plane. Let me be quick to state that I would be the last person to disparage anyone for such fear. I have never met anyone who does not fear *something,* and I have a certain irrational fear myself that causes me to have empathy with people who likewise have "silly" fears.

For the friend who is afraid of flying I found a beautifully reassuring verse, Deuteronomy 33:27: "The eternal God is thy refuge, and underneath are the everlasting arms."

Underneath what? Underneath wherever we are: in the jumbo jet cruising 37,000 feet high or in the submarine in the depths of the sea. In her book *It Takes More Than the Moon,* Mary Irwin described her fears as her astronaut husband blasted off for his walk on the moon. But well she knew that God would be with Jim in Apollo 14. And He was—from countdown to splashdown. The eternal God, our refuge, is always underneath.

I have seen what that assurance can do for a fear-ridden traveler. On at least one occasion I have known the passenger to step aboard, clutching not only her boarding pass but that verse written on a scrap of paper. Also, some have told me that saying the verse over and over calms them when otherwise the journey would have been a nightmare. That should not surprise us, for God's Word *is* living, and it is powerful to meet our need whatever we are "under." Well might we sing with William O. Cushing: "Under His wings I am safely abiding."

There is no greater source of inner security.

125

God has not promised to keep the Christian from all trials. He has promised to be with us in trouble. And trouble frequently means the absence of safety. For example, we drive on icy highways or in dense fog. God does not supernaturally intervene for the Christian driver. But He can, if we will trust Him, provide the sense of security we need for the conditions we face.

If security meant always being safe, would not that call for God's protecting every Christian from any and all harm and danger? I believe He does many times, but not always. On one occasion, violent rainstorms in Texas weakened a church so that its roof caved in during a worship service. A nine-year-old child died and about forty others were injured.

I live in what is commonly called "earthquake country." How well I recall the last big earthquake in the Los Angeles region, February 9, 1971. The jolt that wakened me around 6:00 A.M. The neighbors checking on each other's safety and bemoaning the various breakages as things fell or were tossed about. The chimneys that crashed, blocking access to our driveway and damaging cars as the bricks landed. Worse, the radio reports of many deaths as a hospital wing was demolished.

I remember, too, waiting for the aftershocks that can be as severe or more so than the quake itself. Sitting on my bed, I wrote down some of my feelings during those minutes that seemed like hours. I wanted to leave for my family words of assurance that I had perfect peace, inner security, even in the midst of an earthquake. I was graphically reminded of Psalm 46:1-2: "God is our refuge and strength.

. . . Therefore will not we fear, though the earth be removed."
I do not mean that I shall never feel insecure or fearful.
But I do know that an earthquake did not rob me of peace.

In that disaster Christians as well as non-Christians suffered, some death and others serious material losses. The
fact that God's people were not spared reminds us of Job's
conclusion, "Shall we receive good at the hand of God,
and shall we not receive evil?"

So if our security depends on our always being safe from
harm, we had better forget that security.

"Nevertheless the foundation of God standeth sure. . .
The Lord knoweth them that are His" and He has an am-
ple supply of security to keep us in times of stress.

The Value of Right Remembering

There is more than one way to learn, and sometimes it
takes the negative to drive home the positive. For example,
what is one way of encouraging *insecurity*? Remembering
things that robbed us of security. Letting our mind dwell on
some incident that created feelings of fear, inferiority, or
doubt—all debilitating emotions. We never remember those
without affecting ourselves negatively.

Remembering the negatives is, in a sense, feeding such
feelings.

Likewise, we can build our inner security by remembering the good things that have happened and tracing God's
hand in them.

Again and again in the Old Testament, God's people
were exhorted to remember how God had delivered and led
them (see Deuteronomy 7:18; 8:2; 15:15; 32:7).

It would be a profitable exercise to use a concordance and

127

then read and meditate on the "rememberings." For those were not mental exercises suggested for the purpose of keeping the brain functioning sharply. Inherent in the remembering of former things was the heart-warming encouragement *God will do it again; He who has delivered will deliver; He who has led will continue to lead His people.*

We can similarly look back with profit on our own years, on all the way the Lord has led *us.* In retrospect, I have sometimes wondered, *How did I ever make it through those circumstances that at the time seemed totally unbearable.* The answer is: God was with me. He kept me.

Remembering His goodness in the past, logically I should have no problem in trusting the Lord for my future. But like many another I shrink from a potentially difficult experience, thinking, *I could never go through that.*

How much better, as we read in 1 Samuel 7:12, to "raise [our] Ebenezer" (Ebenezer: "Hitherto the Lord has helped us"). Herein lies the solid foundation of inner security. For the God who helped us in the past is the changeless God (see Malachi 3:6). The New Testament underscores that truth for us in Hebrews 13:8: "Jesus Christ, the same yesterday, and today, and for ever."

How Insecurity Affects Our Daily Lives

Any time we do not avail ourselves of the sustenance God's Word affords us, we are diminishing our chances for the best kind of life here on earth. And that can show up in a variety of ways.

Insecure people have *difficulty believing in* others. They see genuine offers of friendship, for instance, and consider the one who offers it as "having an angle," or "getting something out of it." Thus they rob themselves. Ultimately such people have difficulty in trusting God, taking God and His promises for what they really are, and enjoying a close relationship with the Lord.

Personally I take great comfort in Psalm 56:3, "What time I am afraid, I will trust." Why do I set such store by that verse when I have occasion to feel afraid? *Because it works for me.* It worked the last time I depended upon it, and the time before, and the time before that. Note that trusting is an act of the will. "I *will* trust." The older I get the more convinced I become that we do nothing apart from *willing* to do it. God gives us the resources in Christ that enable us to trust, but we must do the trusting. The Lord may not remove the cause(s) of our fear, but He has promised to deliver us from fear itself. The psalmist writes, "I sought the Lord, and He . . . delivered me from all my fears" (Psalm 34:4).

Another form that insecurity takes is *cynicism.*

The person who is not putting his trust in Christ and enjoying the daily benefits of inner security that such trust brings frequently has a cynical attitude toward God.

Not long ago I was with a group of Christians around a lunch table, and the conversation turned to the topic of security (today's press provides constant fodder for such discussion). At one point someone mentioned Romans 8:28. A person at the table almost sneered as he questioned, "Is *that* still in the Bible?" And we were off on a consideration of "all things work together for good to them that love God." Some began to relate specific instances. But the cynic was not impressed. He linked negative experiences with Romans 8:28. Then to my delight and not mine only, another man broke in with a convincing, "They've worked together for good for me for *sixty years*!"

The sixty-year-old's tone left no doubt in our minds that, for him, Romans 8:28 would work for the rest of his life. It was refreshing to encounter such vibrant faith. That man had no problem of inner insecurity.

To be sure, not everything works for good immediately. "Nevertheless afterward" (as we read in Hebrews 12:11), we see what God is doing for our eventual good.

Insecurity and the joy of the Lord can never go together.

The insecure Christian is so filled with fears, worries, and nameless anxiety, that there is no room in his heart for a joyous outlook on life. He may be devout, he may read the Bible, memorize verses, pray, and be utterly faithful in church attendance, but the joy is missing. I remember such people from those earlier days when churches frequently had "testimony times." There were some whose testimony could be predicted with one-hundred percent accuracy: "I've failed Him many times. But He has never failed me." There was in that as much joy as there is in a lament.

As a new Christian I did not need anybody to tell me something was not right about such a testimony. Certainly it is no tribute to God. True, He never fails us, and He never will. But is it not His purpose that we grow beyond perennial failures? And does not such a regular admission say not, "I have failed Him," but, "I am a failure"?

It is good for us to internalize the truth that God will never fail us, then move on into success experiences with Him. Realization that God has never failed me should be a supreme source of security.

That deep security has never been better defined than in the lovely Swedish hymn:

> More secure is no one ever
> Than the loved ones of the Saviour.

Every stanza breathes encouragement and security in God's promises, culminating in:

> What He takes or what He gives us
> Shows the Father's love so precious;
> We may trust His purpose wholly—
> 'Tis His children's welfare solely.
>
> LINA SANDELL BERG

IT PAYS TO BE SIMPLE

When our Lord was looking around for a model of those who would enter His kingdom, He chose a little child (see Matthew 18:1-3). It is my belief that we never quite learn where our security lies until we can simply trust, like a child. And that is a lesson we are sometimes slow to learn.

I used to think I was trusting the Lord when I was going through some trial, but many times I was also offering suggestions to the Most High as to how He might solve my problem. I am learning how wrong and foolish that is. God is infinitely creative and innovative. He can and does set up situations we could never arrange on our own.

For example, last year I had a seminar scheduled in northeast India. Because of a plane mixup, I arrived one day late. That was the culmination of a series of faith-testing delays, and my trust was at the "help thou my unbelief" point. I stepped off the plane in a part of the world where I did not

131

know one soul. The day before, the coordinator of the seminar had driven four and one-half hours over the mountains to meet me. But now I was alone to fumble through the airport red tape in that sensitive Assam border area.

Finally, with mixed feelings I boarded a bus pointed out to me. Destination, *Meghalaya*. I had never heard of it. Some two hours into the beautiful mountains, the bus stopped, as does everything in that part of the world, for tea. I was sitting by myself in the little roadside tea shop when, hesitantly, two men approached me, and one asked, "Are you Mrs. Lockerbie?" (I can still hardly believe it.) Amazed, I said yes, and both men relaxed and smiled. That had been an unheard-of thing: men in that culture do not speak in public to a woman—a stranger and a foreigner at that.

"I know your daughter, Jeannie, in Bangladesh," one of them explained. Later he told my daughter, "I didn't think she could be your mother because you are tall and she is not." So they had almost decided not to approach me. But God did not let that happen.

Who were the two men?

Both had come from Assam in time for the seminar, only to find I had not arrived. Some of the others believed they should just give up—that I had not been permitted to come to the area. One missionary, however, insisted they should all come back at the same hour the next day. So, with a free day, the two would-be writers boarded a bus to spend the day in a city near where I had landed. Was it a coincidence that their bus coming from the opposite direction stopped at precisely the same time and place that mine did? I think not. Quickly they were able to assure me of two things I needed to know: (1) The bus was taking me to where I was

132

supposed to go, and (2), the seminar group would still be there.

I could now revel with a peace-filled mind in the beauty of Meghalaya ("the abode of the clouds"). And the following day when we all got together, it was with a special sense that the Lord was in all our planning. What a worthwhile time we had!

Later on that trip when still other travel problems developed, I could be quite lighthearted over them. I knew the Lord had the solutions all worked out ahead of time.

So I am learning that it pays to have a simple trust and not to be full of, "Why, Lord?" Does not the Bible teach that "the LORD preserveth the simple"? (Psalm 116:6).

When we have in simple childlike faith tested and proved the promises of God, we *can know* the plus of inner security.

12

BUT YOU DON'T UNDERSTAND:

The Plus of an Understanding Heart

We do not have to be very old to sense the worth of a person with an understanding heart.

My grandaughter, Ellyn, was just a third-grader. School was soon to start, and she wrote me about it. Something in that letter lingered in my mind.

"I don't know if my new teacher is nice," she wrote, and a little of her anxiety came through to me. She explained, "None of my friends have had her. She's just coming to our school this year. So nobody can tell me if she is nice or not."

Having a teacher who was nice was obviously important to that little girl, I could tell. So I found myself questioning, *What exactly does Ellyn mean? What is "nice" as it pertains to the relationship between a young pupil and the teacher with whom the child spends so many hours?* In search of understanding, I queried a number of boys and girls. The answers were varied, but it was evident that the topic had high priority with those who told me of their feelings.

A nine-year-old summed it all up in these few words, "Nice means the teacher understands us kids."

"What do you mean by 'understands'?" I further probed.

"Well—." The boy scratched his head and screwed up

135

his face, then with a bright smile he told me, "I have a nice teacher. He makes me feel comfortable because he understands kids."

Who knows? Perhaps that teacher and others like him pray Solomon's prayer on a continuing basis, the request that God would give them understanding hearts.

Not only children but also adults appreciate the person with an understanding heart. How often we hear one neighbor say of another, "She's so understanding."

What is that quality, and why is it seemingly so rare (if it were not, we would not comment on it when we come across an understanding person).

It is easy to say, "I understand." We all do it, sometimes unthinkingly, and with hurt to the one to whom we say it.

Have you found yourself feeling resentful and angry when someone has said, "I understand," and you were in a position to know the person could not possibly understand? Your reaction may be justified. On the other hand, some well-meaning, warm-hearted friend, relative, or neighbor may just not know what to say and so stumble into, "Oh, I understand." At other times, saying to a hurting person, "I understand" (when you cannot from experience) is akin to saying, "That's the end of that. Let's change the subject."

How well I recall a time when I became angry myself over such a situation. While riding along with some dear friends, I was brooding over a very bad experience I had just gone through. I was poor company for my friends or myself. At one point one of the others reached over from the front seat to where I was in the back and said gently, "I understand." I can remember my retort, "No, you don't!" (which was true.) Almost immediately I felt strong anger at myself for

136

my ungracious and unchristian response. *How could I ever say such a thing?* I thought, feeling more guilty every minute. I certainly did not like myself for my ugly attitude.

I still do not feel justified for my words on that occasion. But I do have a little more insight into what prompted them. The soothing "I understand" had in it (all unwittingly, I am sure) an element of the "shush, shush, now" with which we try to silence a child. I could not have articulated it at the time, but I now realize that I did not want to hear, "I understand," with its close-the-door, let's-change-the-subject connotation. I needed someone to say at that time something like, "Is something troubling you? Would you like to talk about it?" When that was not forthcoming, the result was anger at the friend, then anger at myself, and a strong feeling of guilt. Certainly it was not the result intended by the kind person who said, "I understand."

Nevertheless, we can have true empathy with a person undergoing a trial only when we have been similarly tried or afflicted. For example, the mother who has stood over a tiny casket is in a strategic position to say to one who is undergoing such a trial, "I understand."

Some years ago we received a telephone call from a distraught young doctor telling us their baby—just hours old—had died and asking if I would visit his wife. They were new Christians, and I recognized that the tragedy could be a blow to their faith as well as being heart-breaking. But what could I say to that young mother whose arms were aching from emptiness. Nothing in my own experience gave me anything viable to say to her. Oh, I could read and quote from the Bible; I could pray with her. And those are both relevant

137

and powerful at such times. But would they reach her in that hour of need?

To my mind came another family to whom a similar tragedy had come a year or so earlier. I asked that lovely young woman if she would go with me, and she willingly consented, taking with her some reading matter that had particularly helped her. Although it reopened her own wounds, she shared with the young mother whose baby had just died the very things that had comforted her in the same situation. There was no, "You'll feel better after a while"; no, "Just try to forget and go on living." Rather, after a time of listening, talking, and crying together, we took the grief, the sorrow, and the burden of pain to the One who is the "Man of sorrows and acquainted with grief," the great Comforter.

Why We Should Show Understanding

Sometimes it is very difficult for people who have suffered deep grief to enter into another's present sorrow. They may not want to reopen partly healed wounds.

"I'm just getting over it myself," they may say, "and I don't want to bring it all back."

It is understandable that they do not want to disturb the soothing layers time has spun over their sorrow. We would not judge them for that. But, by so doing, they may withhold from someone who desperately needs it the greatest of all human therapy, genuine, empathetic understanding born of personal experience.

Even so that help is not always forthcoming. Many people have to depend upon professional counselors—sometimes noncaring persons—for help in overcoming devastating emotional crises in their lives. A missionary had lost her husband, not through death, but because he had left her for another woman. A close friend appealed to another Christian who had suffered the same loss, asking that she gently step in with help and comfort. Her response? None. Later she admitted to the one who had made the request, "It was too personal, too private. I didn't want to expose myself in order to help someone else. And I missed out on the chance to be God's channel."

Obviously, that woman had temporarily forgotten that Christians have a mandate to comfort one another (2 Corinthians 1:3-4): "What a wonderful God we have . . . the one who so wonderfully comforts and strengthens us in our hardships and trials. And why does He do this? So that when others are troubled, needing our sympathy and encouragement, we can pass on to them this same help and comfort God has given us (TLB).

Unwillingness is not the only reason some people withhold expressions of comfort, or slough off the other person's problem. It may be that they are signaling, "I have enough troubles of my own. I can't handle yours and mine too." Sometimes that comes out in the seemingly callous, "It's just one of those things."

How Can We Appropriately Express Understanding?

Because the Bible exhorts us to be comforters, we should be—but with honesty. By admitting that we do not understand—that we have not experienced the same sorrow or problem—we may cause the stricken person to believe, *Here is someone who really does care.*

139

A friend with whom I discussed this subject told me about her experience when an office colleague's husband died.

"I just went up to her and put my arm around her and said, 'You know, Alice, that I can't understand what you're going through. The Lord has never called me to suffer such a trial. But I want you to know that I love you—I care about what happens to you—and I'm praying everyday for you.' She squeezed both my hands, thanking me for not just saying, 'I understand.'"

The bereaved woman had then opened up and talked, as the healing tears flowed. And there had been no anger.

I am not saying that unless I have suffered the loss of a loved one, I should never attempt to speak a word of comfort and solace to one who is bereaved; that if I have not known bitter disappointment and disillusionment, I would do better to keep quiet in the presence of another's distress. It is *how* we say what we say that makes the difference. So it is good for us to pray before coming out with our platitudes, however well meant. For instance, saying, "Time will heal," offers no comfort, for the person cannot hurry time and thus speed the healing process. Moreover, time does not heal; *God* heals in the process of time.

Nor is it inappropriate to say that you have gone through certain trials. But it is more considerate not to dwell on or elaborate on these. It is better to relate how faithful God was to you during the trouble, but even that has to be stated with sensitivity. Sometimes the hurting Christian's need is for a human listening ear; he needs someone who will bear with him through repeated recitals of his grief and what caused it. And the understanding person will never remind him, "You've told me that before." Saying that is like urging the grieving person to "forget it and cheer up; I got over my problem, now you get over yours." It is like putting a Band-Aid on a cancer.

Fortunately for humanity there are still those admirable individuals who do understand, who have "sat where we sit" (see Ezekiel 3:15). They have known suffering similar to our own, and when they reach out with comfort, there is reality in it. Also once in a while we come across an individual who, though he or she may not necessarily have suffered a great deal, appears to have remarkable insight into other people's problems and need for understanding. Generally those are not the quick-answer people, who have solutions to all the ills of the world, including yours and mine, on the tips of their tongues.

A characteristic of understanding is unselfishness. The self-centered person cannot, seemingly, emotionally afford to reach out to another's grief. That may be due, of course, to his own need to talk. Because most of us like to talk and be listened to, deliberately refraining from doing so in the interests of a more needy friend or neighbor is true unselfishness—and a hallmark of an understanding heart.

The Source of an Understanding Heart

It is intriguing to me that of all the available options, Solomon asked for an understanding heart. With the *certainty of having your wish granted,* what would you have asked for? The reasoning that Solomon as king had everything his heart could desire is fallacious thinking. For even the most fabulously wealthy, there are always the unreachables. In man's thinking, "enough" is generally "more than I have."

141

The request for an understanding heart must have pleased God in Solomon's day; undoubtedly it still pleases Him.

Understanding would appear to be a special attribute that God gives certain people. From my own observation those are individuals who have a mission in life to serve the Lord and to help humanity. So, initially, such people have made a commitment to God. Dr. Ralph Byron has said he specifically asked God for wisdom not only to reach the unsaved around him but to teach Christians so that they will grow and mature in the Christian life. But Dr. Byron's prior request was that God would let him serve as a man standing "in the gap" (Ezekiel 22:30).

Dr. Clyde Narramore says he can pinpoint the day God gave him the promise "I will give you a mouth and wisdom" (Luke 21:15).

Wisdom and understanding are closely allied. Sometimes we speak of a person as having "native wisdom." By that we generally mean that such wisdom comes from other than formal learning; and almost always the connotation is that the person also has great understanding of other people.

We rob ourselves and others we might be able to help when we fail to avail ourselves of the wisdom that only God can give: *priceless* wisdom, as we read in Job 28. In verse 12 Job asks, "Where shall wisdom be found?" Then he goes into a description of the worth of wisdom, placing it high above gold, silver, or rubies. Again in verse 20 he asks, "Whence then cometh wisdom? and where is the place of understanding?"—questions he answers in verse 28. "The fear of the Lord, that is wisdom; and to depart from evil is understanding."

In the New Testament, the practical James tells us how

142

we obtain wisdom: "If any of you lack wisdom, let him ask of God, that giveth to all men liberally . . . and it shall be given him" (James 1:5).

Whatever our personal need for empathy and understanding, we must go to our all-wise, omniscient Lord. Elisha Hoffman, hymnwriter, could have been speaking for all of us when he wrote:

> I must tell Jesus all of my trials;
> .   .   .   .
> Jesus can help me, Jesus alone.

The disciples knew this. Grieved over the horrible, untimely death of John the Baptist, they "went and told Jesus" (Matthew 14:12). And can you hear Peter's poignant, "Lord, to whom shall we go?" (John 6:68).

Because the Lord Jesus knows all about us, He will never offer less than the comfort we need. He has no stock answers. As we develop more understanding, we will realize that stock sympathetic phrases have little value, and we will seek rather to share something of the wisdom God is teaching us. We may not always understand, but we can hope to be supportive and comforting when someone near us is hurting.

BECAUSE WE ARE ALL DIFFERENT

One of the glories of being human is that we are uniquely made. God does not deal in carbon copies; we each are His one-of-a-kind creation. That affects many aspects of our lives. Often we view the same thing differently. What one grieving person can accept as understanding from someone may make another person feel deeply resentful. How good, then, to know that God has no "comfort kits," prepackaged to meet generalized needs, to be dispensed for anything and everything.

Perhaps, as those who genuinely intend to be helpful, we need to guard against insensitivity along this line, thinking, *What was right for Anne's needs will be effective in helping Mary.* That is not necessarily so. I know a fine-intentioned widow who has seemingly adjusted to the loss of her husband and consequently goes around dispensing "what helped me" as the sole answer to coping with the death of one's mate. Certainly she is to be commended for wanting to be helpful. The snag is that she has a prescribed "grief recovery process" all worked out in "steps." And she expects (requires) of others in similar circumstances that they fit in, act, and react as she did—*and do it on time,* that is, be at Step 3 on schedule.

God does not expect that we will all heal at the same pace or as a result of the same therapy. He knows our frame, the Bible tells us (Psalm 103:13). He knows we are all different. And if we ask Him, He will give us the insight we need to be truly helpful.

A great plus for us is that we have the indwelling Comforter, the Holy Spirit Himself, to guide us and to teach us to be comforters.

It is good to utilize one of the basic ingredients of an understanding heart, *careful listening.* There are many ways to "listen," and the person who is talking out hurt and grief in the hope of being understood and finding help, can all too quickly discern if we are indeed listening. We listen with our eyes and our bodily gestures as well as with our ears.

In conclusion, we must also respect *confidentiality*. That will keep us from peddling information that has been shared by one who trusts us to be both understanding and above gossip.

A worthwhile prayer to begin our day might be this:

> Lord, please give me the wisdom and the understanding I need hour by hour today. You know what my day will hold. Please keep me close to You and make me sensitive to the hurting people I shall meet. I really want to have an understanding heart, Lord.

The God who was pleased to answer Solomon's prayer will hear and grant yours and mine.

We might one day be surprised to hear of ourselves, "She [he] is such an *understanding* person."

13

LIVING IS FOR NOW:

The Plus of the Present

One of the most direct statements in the Bible is, "Behold, now is the accepted time" (2 Corinthians 6:2). Although referring to an eternal decision, that verse is also potent with regard to temporal things.

THE VITAL IMPORTANCE OF NOW

Because, in addition to being the "accepted time," now is the *only* time we have, we should do what we need to do and *do it now.* Just three little words, but how significant they can be.

Sometimes we have special cause to be thankful that we have activated an impulse to "do it now."

I recall the good feeling I had when I opened a letter from someone who was interested in Christian writing. The letter was from a minister I had known in his student days. He took time to explain why he had written. A heart ailment had taken him out of the active ministry, and he was planning to serve the Lord through the written word. He asked me for some tips.

I am no better than anyone else at replying speedily to every letter I receive. I do not know why I answered that

147

particular one so promptly. But I did, offering some encouragement and practical suggestions. Barely one week had elapsed when I received another, that time from the minister's wife. "Thank you so much for your good letter to David," she wrote, and added, "The Lord took him home last night."

Even as my heart went out to that new widow, I realized that God was speaking to my own heart. How glad I was that I had taken time to reply at once, rather than putting off, even though the Lord knew that old friend had no further need for human help and encouragement.

If the experience just related would say anything, it is that now is the time. How often I feel special delight over just a brief note saying, "I was thinking about you, but how will you know if I don't tell you?" And there may be only another sentence or two. By contrast, we tend to put off "till we can write a nice long letter"—and frequently nothing happens. What if we have offended or wronged someone, and we delay, possibly waiting for the other to make the first move. Or we are waiting for "the right time." There is no remorse so keen as that caused by knowing we have neglected to do something and now it is too late. The opportunity is gone forever.

What if the Holy Spirit is gently nudging us to go and present the gospel to a shut-in or an unchurched neighbor? Isn't now the time to do it? Not often does God *dramatically* remind us of the uncertainty of life—that today is ours, and tomorrow may be too late. But common sense and practicality echo that it is so.

"No time like the present," we quote to each other. A cliché, I know. But clichés become clichés because they contain an element of truth. "No time like the present" is a worthwhile precept, and putting precept into practice can often be accomplished just by heeding the three little words *Do it now*.

How often it is not the actual tasks themselves that tire us out, but the image they conjure up in our minds. "I have to do this—and this—and this"—and a mountain of jobs blurs our vision of the two or three we could be doing while we are sighing over those that are waiting to be done. It is somehow easier for us to lament, "There's so much to do," than to get busy and attack things one at a time. Yet there is great satisfaction in seeing the slate come clean of "things to do today."

One day when I had just completed a list of To Do's, I was about to sigh over it, but this much better thought occurred to me: *What if I had nothing to do? What if nobody needed me to do anything? Would I be happier?* The answer was simple: there is no happiness, no fulfillment in doing nothing and in feeling not needed.

So that day I thanked the Lord for giving me reasons for being alive, and the strength, energy, and soundness of mind to get at my list instead of moaning over it.

In every area of life the three little words *Do it now,* when acted upon, can have a salutary effect. One need not hold a degree in administration in order to be fairly well organized. And, because being a Christian is something that should affect our attitudes and behavior in everyday living, we do well to call to mind that "God is not the author of confusion, but of peace" (1 Corinthians 14:33). Although the frame of reference is different, the message is the same. We can know a greater sense of peace when we are not frus-

149

trated by the undone things that nag our consciences.

A proved way to help us implement our resolve to "do it now" is to make that a matter of daily prayer. Let us tell the Lord we have a problem along that line and ask Him to strengthen our determination. God will enable anyone who really wants to, to *do it now,* for now is the only time we are sure of.

PUTTING A BURDEN ON TOMORROW

Tomorrow is built on today, as a second story is built upon a first. Keeping that in mind can motivate us to make today count.

> Not yesterday's load we are called on to bear,
> Nor the morrow's uncertain and shadowy care;
> Why should we look forward or back with dismay?
> Our needs, as our mercies, are but for the day.
> One day at a time, and the day is His day;
> He has numbered its hours, though they haste or delay.
> His grace is sufficient; we walk not alone;
> As the day, so the strength that He giveth His own.
>
> ANNIE JOHNSON FLINT

One reason (or excuse) we offer for not letting or making today be all it can be is the little word *if.* "If I just knew what tomorrow will bring," I hear people say. And there are many who are ready and willing to cater to such a wish. There has never been a day when daily newspapers, monthly magazines, talk-show personalities and others have offered a greater variety of promised glimpses into the future through horoscopes, and so on. Even Christians, who have the Bible's prohibitions against such things, are becoming ensnared.

150

One young woman admitted to me, "I've gotten so that I'm not as interested in my morning devotions as I used to be, and I can't wait to see my horoscope in the morning paper."

The desire to see into the future is a universal yearning. But it is not for us to see beyond today. A more heart-satisfying outlook is:

> God holds the key of all unknown,
> And I am glad;
> If other hands should hold the key,
> Or if He trusted it to me,
> I might be sad.
>
> J. PARKER

I also like this little gem I came across in a *Holiday Inn* magazine (December 1970): "Go as far as you can see, and when you get there you will be able to see farther."

To me that savors of daily walking "in the light" and of God's Word that is "a light unto my path" (1 John 1:7; Psalm 119:105).

WHAT MAKES US SO TOMORROW-ORIENTED?

It helps to know *why* we do what we do.

The matter of putting off today in favor of tomorrow begins early. By various means we are receiving signals that tomorrow is better than today can be. The small child hears, "Wait till you're bigger," or "You're too young yet." He views his school-age brother or sister as possibly "having arrived." The ten-year-old can hardly wait to get into his teens; the teenager longs for the "freedom" of the adults—and so on. Always something beyond today creates a conscious or unconscious dissatisfaction with what is right now.

151

Meanwhile the elderly are too often looking back, drawn in memory to "the good old days"—which may or may not have been "good" at the time. So they, also, are missing out on what awareness of each day in itself can offer.

Looking back on some of those earlier days, I have to admit that I did not always value them for their own worth. Then, as now, we all tended to have greater expectations of tomorrow than of today—and not always happy ones. There were then, and there are still, those who are so busy saving for a rainy tomorrow that they cannot enjoy the good weather today.

People of all ages and conditions sigh, saying, "If this month ever gets over—" Or, "When spring finally comes—"

Nothing is wrong with such anticipation, as long as it is *not taking the place of living today.*

All of us have certain traits, idiosyncrasies, or whatever we want to call them. One of mine (and you may recognize it as yours, too) is that I am happiest when I have something to look forward to. Usually in my case it is a meaningful trip (I nearly always have a suitcase partially packed). But the prospect of a leisurely lunch or dinner with a special friend works the same magic, though to a lesser degree.

Unless carried to excess, it is perfectly all right to find joy in anticipation. Excessive dwelling on the future can, however, be unhealthy. I was meditating on that some time ago. Let me share with you some of my thoughts: *Why do I need something in the future to spice my today? What is lacking in the day's own offerings, its possibilities for fulfillment? How much may dissatisfaction with the present contribute to my greater expectations of tomorrow?*

As a result of considering those and kindred possibilities,

I began to have a greater appreciation of "This is the day which the Lord has made; we [I] will rejoice and be glad in it." Inherent in that is tacit acceptance of the fact that the supply and demands of the day will balance each other. Our heavenly Father knows what we have need of, the Bible tells us. And, like the manna in the wilderness, there is daily provision of our needs.

To let oneself overly depend on tomorrow is a form of folly. To do so defeats happiness and productivity today. And have you thought that in being future-minded you may actually be squandering today's resources?

If I do less than I can do today (because I am trusting in tomorrow), I am being wasteful with God's promised strength (Deuteronomy 33:25). Nor can I bank it or otherwise retain it. One day's strength for one day's needs is obviously the message God gives us. Neither can we mortgage tomorrow's portion, or we undoubtedly would at times. That calls to mind my Scottish grandmother whom I remember as always knitting. We were not Christians, but there was still a strong reverence for "the Sabbath."

When on occasion the family Saturday night gathering lasted late, Grandma, still knitting, was sure to say as the clock struck midnight, "I'll just borrow an hour off the Lord." But we cannot do that.

In his book *You Are Never Alone* (Revell), Dr. Charles L. Allen writes:

> The only real time that we have to live, to be, and to act, is the present. Neither has any birth or any death ever happened yesterday or tomorrow. Birth and death and everything else that is important, happens right now.

153

For our day to be worthwhile for itself, we have to take care of the minutes. As we sometimes sing:

> Give ev'ry flying minute
> Something to keep in store.
> ANNIE L. COGHILL

And because our words and actions echo our thoughts, we need to start with right thinking.

HOW WE CAN ENJOY TODAY

How can we set about to enjoy today for itself and not just as a calendar stop on the way to another day, a "better" day?

Each of us will find his own way to overcome that imbalance if he recognizes it as such. But as a suggestion, let me share with you something I recall having heard Dr. Clyde Narramore say to his staff one morning early in December: "Let's begin to enjoy Christmas today; we don't have to wait till Christmas Eve or Christmas Day to enjoy the beauty of the carols and the whole "spirit of Christmas." That was thinking in the present tense. As that word of wisdom comes back to my mind, I can see what such thinking can do for us. At Christmas it can help prevent the frustration, the tension that so often builds up in what should be the happiest season of the year (or one of two happiest: Easter is equally joyous for the Christian, for what is one without the other?).

As we let ourselves each day become aware of the beauty, love, and compassion that is still in our world if we would but look for it, we will not have to postpone enjoyment until some peak day in the future. Too often when we focus all our hopes for happiness on one particular event or one spe-

154

cial day, we are programming ourselves for possible disillusionment. We are putting too great a burden on that one day or one happening.

Anyway, tomorrow may not come. It does not always come for everybody.

We may enjoy singing, "God's tomorrow is a day of gladness." Meanwhile, it is good to keep in mind that so is *God's today*. For today is God's gift to us—every day. And each day can be lived on the plus side.

Moody Press, a ministry of the Moody Bible Institute, is designed for education, evangelization, and edification. If we may assist you in knowing more about Christ and the Christian life, please write us without obligation: Moody Press, c/o MLM, Chicago. Illinois 60610.